HUMOR IN ART

HUMOR IN ART
A Celebration of Visual Wit

NICHOLAS ROUKES

Davis Publications, Inc.
Worcester, Massachusetts

Copyright © 1997
Davis Publications, Inc.
Worcester, Massachusetts U.S.A.

Publisher: Wyatt Wade
Editorial Director: Helen Ronan
Production Editor: Nancy Wood Bedau
Manufacturing Coordinator: Steven Vogelsang
Copyeditor: Frankie Wright
Design: Janis Owens
Assistant Production Editor: Carol Harley
Editorial Assistance: Jane Boland, Colleen Fitzpatrick, Stacie Moffat

Library of Congress Catalog Card Number: 96-086386

ISBN: 0-87192-304-1

10 9 8 7 6 5 4 3 2

Printed in China

Cover:
Craig Nutt, *We Will Never Use Food as a Weapon (Carrot Bomb),* 1989. Oil paint on carved tupelo and poplar, 24" x 15" x 20" (61 x 38 x 50.8 cm). Photo: Ricky Yanura © Craig Nutt.

Halftitle, p. i:
This print is a satire against the excessive burden of taxation levied at the British public in the late 1700s. William Pitt, the politician-showman, draws John Bull's attention to a peep show and picks his pocket.

Isaac Cruikshank, *The Raree Show* (also known as *John Bull En-lighten'd*), 1797. Location unknown.

Frontispiece:
Rogers, a carpenter by trade, began carving only after his retirement. His three-dimensional tableaus are inspired by dreams and the supernatural, and feature motifs of vampires, ghosts, and "haints" (the nonliving).

Sultan Rogers, *Haint House,* 1987. Wood and paint, 6½" x 3" x 3" (16.5 x 7.6 x 7.6 cm). Courtesy of the New Orleans Museum of Art, collection of Warren and Sylvia Lowe.

Back cover art:
Anne Coe, *Migrating Mutants,* 1986, Acrylic on canvas, 61" x 61" (154.9 x 154.9 cm). Horwitch Newman Gallery, Scottsdale, Arizona.

For Julie

This book is also dedicated to Thalia, the muse of wit and humor—and the legion of visual artists who are illumined by her divine charity.

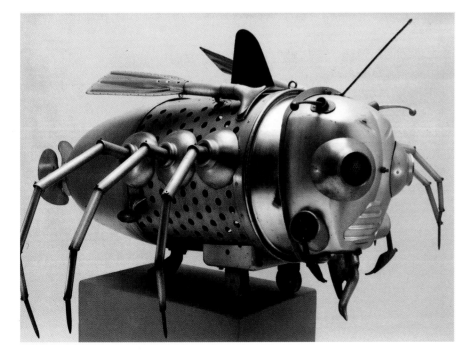

The comic robot sculptures created by Bailey seem to exude a pleasant domesticity. Perhaps this is because of their memory of their past lives as appliances and kitchenware.

Clayton Bailey, *Ro-bug,* 1980. Found objects, 40" x 50" x 24" (101.6 x 127 x 61 cm). Courtesy of the artist.

Acknowledgments

My most sincere thanks to the artists, writers, museum and gallery directors, psychologists, humorologists, and theorists who have provided inspiration and material for the research and production of this book.

I am grateful for the counsel of Roberta Loach and the cooperation of Charles Miller, John Natsoulas, Walter Askin, Nicolas Treadwell, Peter Joseph, and David Gilhooly. My special thanks to the editorial staff of Davis Publications, particularly to my editors Helen Ronan and Nancy Bedau, and to copyeditor Frankie Wright and designer Janis Owens. A special thank you to assistants Carol Harley and Colleen Fitzpatrick.

Finally, to you, my reader, I extend an open invitation for your thoughts and contributions for possible inclusion in subsequent editions of *Humor in Art.*

For information regarding lectures on visual humor, write to the author, care of the publisher, or e-mail nroukes@ucalgary.ca

Carved by Haida peoples of the Northwest Coast, ceremonial pipes are not designed to be smoked but are used in Haida mythology and shamanism. In this example, a recumbent man holds the tail of the oyster catcher, which in turn holds tobacco leaves in its beak.

Ornamental Pipe, c. 1820–1850. Argillite (black slate), 11½" (29 cm). Vancouver Centennial Museum.

Facing Page:
Suzanne Adan, *Lust: The Garden of Adan*,
from *The Seven Deadly Sins*, 1991. Linocut,
57¼" x 58½" (145.4 x 148.6 cm). Michael
Himovitz Gallery, Sacramento, California.

Contents

Chapter 3
The Laughing Artist

Below:
These whimsical "hearts" are a result of word-image interplay and punnery. Left to right: *Love in Bloom, Violated Heart, Heart and Soul, Chicken Hearted, These Foolish Things, Sweetheart Joan Baby, A Distressed Heart, Volcanic Heart.*

Jeremy Anderson, *Love in Bloom,* 1977–1978. Wood, styrofoam, acrylic; tallest object 16¾" x 4¼" x 4¼" (42.5 x 10.8 x 10.8 cm). Anderson Family Collection. Photo: Marco P. Zecchin.

> We are the only creatures who both laugh and weep, and I think it's because we are the only creatures who see the difference between the way things are and the way they might be. Tears bring relief, but laughter brings release.
>
> **Robert Fulghum, b. 1937**
>
> **American writer**

Introduction

Look, he's winding up the watch of his wit; by and by it will strike.

William Shakespeare,
The Tempest

Is this an imaginative flight of fantasy or a satirical reference to a world going slightly crazy? Is it surreal or "so-real"? Pratchenko: "The narrative is a loose interpretation of an actual event I witnessed in which the commander of a fleet of vessels in the mid-Atlantic lost his reason and subsequently, his command."

Paul Pratchenko, *Leadership, Destination, Velocity,* 1985. Acrylic, prismacolor, graphite on paper, 29½" x 41½" x 1½" (74.9 x 105.4 x 3.8 cm). Courtesy of the artist.

Whether considered from the viewpoint of the creative potential that it offers the artist, or from the salubrious effect that it has on human behavior in general, humor stands out as something that should be cherished, preserved, and nurtured.

Humor does more than tweak the funny bone and tickle the intellect; with it, we are liberated from the restraints of convention and the weariness and pain of reality. Humor has the power to restore and sustain psychological and physical health.

It is, pure and simple, a universal tonic.

Laughter is the best medicine. Laughter has been heralded as a tonic for human afflictions since the time of Hippocrates. It produces a beneficial effect on blood pressure, respiratory activity, pulmonary oxygenation, metabolism, and cardiovascular health. It relaxes the nervous system and assists the brain's release of endorphins, which are the body's natural painkillers and tension-reducing neuropeptides.

Life with laughter is more fun; you are healthier, learn faster, are a better communicator, and a more enjoyable companion. Furthermore, you are less likely to burn out from stress or what might be called "terminal professionalism."

What makes us laugh, what is funny and why, however, is yet another matter. Humor is an elusive subject that baffles even experts as to the way it should be defined and taught. Though some critics venture to say that too much investigation of the subject will destroy one's capacity to enjoy it, others disagree. Laurence J. Peter, co-author of *The Laughter Prescription*, writes, "On the contrary, there is reason to believe that people's senses of humor have been *heightened* by learning more about the subject. Gaining new knowledge and uses of humor and its application is a safe venture. There is no other activity that can be as rewarding in so many areas of your life." And from psychologist Joel Goodman: "Why should such a beautiful gift be left to chance? The questions we should be asking are these: How can we be more *intentional* about calling on humor in our lives and the lives of others? How can we make *sense* of humor and then *serve* it, or—more accurately—how can it serve us?"

Educators recognize the importance of humor in establishing a positive learning environment in their classrooms. Humor helps to keep students alert and responsive. A good sprinkling of fun and jocularity, mixed in with education, serves as an anxiety regulator, which encourages a freer atmosphere that can bond people together and nurture self-esteem and social empathy.

The reasons for supporting the study and practice of visual humor in the classroom are championed throughout *Humor in Art*. Humor is an intrinsic part of human expression. Humorous art not only offers levity and diversion, but instructs and serves as a means for expressing diverse opinions and emotions, and can address social, moral, and ethical issues. It merits serious study. Teachers should remind students that, aside from comics and other popular arts, the fine arts, too, have a mirthful side.

Students might ask: If humor makes people happy, healthy, and compassionate, and if it serves so well to foster the reception to ideas, why does it seem that there has been so little of it in our museums and

Humor, as an example of the creative act in its full range of potential, or humor as play, is a sensitive means of coping, an adaptive vehicle for making life's compromises and is, therefore, a growth experience.
William F. Fry, Jr., 20th-century psychologist and writer

Askin's comically discordant artworks celebrate nonsense, which pivots on whimsy, displaced logic, eccentric analogy, incongruity, and pseudoprofundity.

Walter Askin, *Untitled Drawing*, 1984. Pen and ink. Courtesy of the artist.

art galleries? Robert Hughes, art critic and author of *Shock of the New* and *Culture of Complaint*, writes that the American art world is in gridlock today because it steadfastly clings to an outdated 1980s star system, which imposes a uniformity of taste that has few parallels in American cultural history. Artist-satirist-critic Roberta Loach has said, "I believe galleries and museums who shy away from humor, especially strong-content satire, are acting either out of ignorance, lack of courage, or fear of losing funding due to a prevailing ultra-conservative and 'politically correct' climate of our time."

Some galleries and museums do value the importance of visual humor. Many are credited throughout this book, and their endorsement of visual humor creates a wider public awareness. Happily, too, there is an international groundswell of interest in humor in art. According to Walter Askin, director of the Visual Humor Project, a worldwide network devoted to making the work of the visual humorist more visible, there is an unprecedented flowering of humorous work by serious artists all over the world. This groundswell is not so unlike the Renaissance tradition, in which laughter was regarded as the people's highest spiritual privilege.

This book celebrates the universe of visual humor in its many modes: whimsy, wit, parody, irony, satire, and nonsense humor. Here you'll encounter a macrocosm of smiles and laughter united in art, a universal language that has the capacity to entertain, interpret, reveal, regenerate, and advocate. *Humor in Art* lauds the artists whose spirited expressions have made the world a better place, and it advocates the value of visual humor in education.

The idea for this book evolved from my research in visual creativity and synectics. (See my two previous publications, *Art Synectics*, 1980, and *Design Synectics*, 1984, published by Davis Publications, Inc., Worcester,

The idiosyncratic amalgamations of form and images are absurd and yet metaphoric, depending on whether the viewer is an optimist or pessimist.

Rand Schiltz, *Renovations, Out with the Old, in with the New*, 1991. Vacuum cast bronze and lacquer, 14" x 11" x 4" (35.5 x 28 x 10.2 cm). Courtesy of the artist.

MA.) *Synectics* means "bringing together different things into unified connection"—a basic tenet in humor as well as in creativity theory.

The art for this book was selected on the basis of conceptual and aesthetic quality, as well as instructive potential. If a picture is worth a thousand words, much can be learned from pictures that words alone cannot convey.

Here's what you'll find in *Humor in Art:*

Chapter One, *Modus Operandi,* provides useful information and insight into the mechanisms by which artists engage comic imagination and kick-start the production of wit and humor.

Chapter Two, *A Legacy of Visual Humor,* traces comic iconography through the ages and highlights some of history's crowning achievements.

Chapter Three, *The Laughing Artist,* describes the genres of visual humor and includes cartooning, a genuine art form in its own right and a unique form of instant communication.

Chapter Four, *Humor That Bites,* sheds light on parody and consciousness-raising satire.

Chapter Five, *A Splendid Chaos,* explains why nonsense humor and comic surrealism do not lack "sense" at all.

In Chapter Six, *Humorobics,* opportunities for indulging in comic imagination are provided through studio and classroom activities. Use this chapter for activity ideas and reference as you read or teach from the earlier chapters, or as you create visual humor in your own studio.

Remember that creativity flourishes when things are done for enjoyment, and what better way to set up a creative environment than with humor.

Whether visual humor, through parody and satire, is directed to the sober task of awakening an apathetic society to its faults and foibles, or is aimed at providing momentary diversion from the world's absurdities, it serves an essential service on both counts. But is humor for everyone? I like writer Anne Wilson Schaef's answer: "Well, maybe not for everyone. It's only for people who want to have fun, enjoy life, and feel alive."

I couldn't agree more.

N.R., Calgary, Alberta, 1996

Fantasy and humor are whimsically linked and evoke an amusing image that alludes to inner emotions.

Karen Breschi, *Grabbed by the Lovebug,* 1994. Mixed media, 76" x 28" x 5" (193 x 71.1 x 12.7 cm). Courtesy of the Braunstein/Quay Gallery, San Francisco. Photo: Don Felton.

Modus Operandi

Chapter 1

Humor, say the pundits, issues from "a growing wisdom." The artist with a sense of humor is a thinking and feeling person who can make leaps of faith and apply free association, witwork, and hand skill to conceive a universe of levity and laughter. Artists ignite humor when they set their mirthful imaginations into motion, when fantasy transforms the ordinary into the extraordinary, and when the expected is exchanged for the unexpected.

Facing Page:
After sixty years in pictures, the legendary film director Billy Wilder makes his debut as a visual artist. An inveterate collector of bric-a-brac, he enlisted sculptor Bruce Houston's help to paraphrase Gertrude Stein's epic prose in three-dimensional form.

Billy Wilder and Bruce Houston, *This Fish Needs a Bicycle*, 1993. Mixed media, 9" x 10" (22.8 x 25.4 cm). Courtesy of the Louis Stern Gallery, Beverly Hills, California. Photo by Brian Forrest.

Fun-damentals of Visual Humor

Artists who create with humor commonly employ a variety of strategies to set the world of reality and the world of fantasy on a collision course. When reality and illusion collide, there arises first a bewilderment at the riddle that is presented, then contemplation, and finally resolution and laughter when the integrating factor—the revealed analogy—is perceived. We also laugh at nonsense—when contemplation reveals the riddle to be nothing more than sheer absurdity, a joke played on our analog-seeking mentality.

Rather than delve deeply into a scientific analysis of humor, this chapter explores ways in which artists transform ordinary subjects into strange and unconventional ones. Nevertheless, to understand what artists do, it helps to understand how humor works.

Mixing realism and fantasy, Brennan changes the normal scale of things in a way that defies logical perception. Note the painting's dimensions (shown actual size). Brennan's miniatures never exceed a few inches square.

Fanny Brennan, *The Visitor*, 1992. Oil on gessoed panel, 2" x 3" (5 x 7.6 cm). Courtesy of Leigh A. Morse, agent for the artist.

Anatomy of Humor

Psychologists point out that humor is clearly, in its cognitive nature, an analog-making process that finds in this characteristic a kinship with all other metaphoric experience, including play, myths, poetry and fairy tales.[1] In this regard, humor theories are similar to creativity theories.

In his book *What's So Funny?*, Murray Davis points out that humor theories have been traditionally classified into three main groups: *incongruity theories*, developed by Kant and Schopenhauer; *release from restraint (tension relief) theories*, from Herbert Spencer and Sigmund Freud; and *superiority theories*, developed by Aristotle and Thomas Hobbes.[2] These three groups reinforce one another by dealing with the same basic complex process: "An individual (1) who perceives humor through 'incongruity,' (2) expresses through laughter the 'release' or 'relief' of being subjectively unaffected by this objective contradiction, and (3) consequently feels his [or her] laughingly sustained subjective integration manifest his 'superiority' to the humorously disintegrated object."[3]

A joke, for example, has discrepant elements that riddle the brain. At first, the joke perplexes with incongruity and demands an intellectual effort to decode the presented anomaly. When the brain finally "gets" the joke, that is, by perceiving an analogy or recognizing the absurdity, it resolves the discrepancy between the incongruent elements—and, at last, closes with laughter.

Every joke, visual or verbal, is a violation of an expectation, an organized collision of distinct elements of distant universes. And because each of us responds differently to a joke, one person's unresolved incongruity may be another's insight.

Then there is the mirthful bicameral brain. Some contemporary theorists believe that the right hemisphere of the brain (the intuitive, perceptual, and creative lobe) may play a critical role in understanding and appreciating humor. As psychologist Paul E. McGhee notes, "It is proposed that simultaneous processing associated primarily with the right hemisphere plays a key role of achieving humorous insights, although

Loach's painting is funny for its outrageous juxtaposition of images, but it gives pause for thoughtful contemplation of its covert satire. The sharks are possibly a metaphor for the ruthless dealers and mean-spirited individuals in the artists' lives. Diego Rivera's portrait is shown on Frida's forehead, a symbol of the influence he had in her life. Frida has borrowed Ulysses' boat to make the journey of self-realization—her own personal odyssey.

Roberta Loach, *The Lonely Odyssey of the Artist, (Homage to Frida Kahlo and Francisco Goya)*, 1995. Acrylic on canvas, 56" x 50" (142.2 x 127 cm). Courtesy of the artist.

Stanley's work synthesizes classical art and mythology and comments on the human condition, with particular reference to family and social issues. Stanley: "*The Functional Family* is an homage to Velasquez's *Las Meninas* and was an excuse to research the Court of Philip IV. In painting this picture, I became obsessed with the portraits of Philip and of Queen Marianna, his second wife."

Louise Stanley, *Functional Family Triptych (Dad's Version)*, 1993. Gouache, 41" x 26" (104.1 x 66 cm). Courtesy of the artist.

AS ASHTRAYS GO, IT WAS CERTAINLY QUITE IMPRESSIVE

With wishful fantasy Baxter alters history, the various laws of nature and science, and, in short, turns the everyday world on its ear. "If it's enigmatic, unsettling, and stops people for a second, that's what I want."

Glen Baxter, *As Ashtrays Go…*, 1992. Pen and ink, panel cartoon. © Glen Baxter, 1992. Courtesy of the artist.

sequential processing associated with the left hemisphere will usually be involved in providing pertinent information necessary for achieving such insights. It is proposed that an optimal balance of right and left hemisphere processing is critical for maximizing the funniness of a joke or cartoon."[4]

Ruffner, Ginny, *Another Way for the Chicken to Cross the Road*, 1994. Glass and mixed media, 17" x 18" x 8" (43.2 x 45.7 x 20.3 cm). Courtesy of the artist.

> If the artist is to invent, there has to be a climate that is not fearful of newness or of irreverence. Invention depends on the freedom to play.
>
> **Virginia Smither, 20th-century American graphic designer**

Incongruity

Surprise, momentary chaos, and incongruity kick-start the production of humor. The incongruous is something that does not make sense. It is anything that is out of harmony with the rational, expected picture we have in our minds of "how things should be."

We laugh the instant we "get" a joke, when we make the connection, no matter how ludicrous or far-fetched, between disparities. We also

The teachings of the Bible have inspired many self-taught artists, such as the Coopers, to depict the struggle between good and evil. Working as a team, Jesse paints what Ronald carves or assembles.

Jesse and Ronald Cooper, *Praising the King: Kerosene Lamp*, 1989. Acrylic on metal, 38" x 17" (96.5 x 43.2 cm). Courtesy of the New Orleans Museum of Art, collection of Gertrude and Ben Caldwell.

laugh when our attempt to resolve an incongruity is foiled, when we realize that there is no logical resolution to a particular anomaly—that we have been fooled by its total nonsense.

Incongruity, the keystone of humor, is welcomed by visual humorists. Unlike the real world with its fixed rules of logic, conduct, and order, humor is based on the liberty to make wacky and irrational analogies and comparisons.

Visual humor in its many forms—whimsy, wit, irony, parody, satire, and nonsense humor—pivots on the way incongruity is structured. The degree of funniness in an attempt at humor depends in part on the quantity and quality of incongruities present and on the responder's familiarity with the expectation system from which the incongruities depart.[5] Whether a particular literary or visual image is perceived as being mildly strange or "off-the-wall" strange depends on the gulf between what is presented and what is already known.

René Magritte's *The Treachery of Images* is a prime example of incongruity in fine art. Magritte presents a painted image of a pipe

The artist plays with viewer perception. He writes on his canvas "This is not a pipe," but what else could it be? Magritte's point was that the pipe is only a representation; it cannot be smoked. "If I had written on my picture, 'this is a pipe,' I'd have been lying!"

René Magritte, *La Trahison des Images (Ceci n'est pas une pipe); The Treachery of Images (This Is Not a Pipe)*, 1928. Oil on canvas, 23⅜" x 37" (60 x 94 cm). Los Angeles County Museum of Art.

accompanied by the words, *Ceci n'est pas une pipe*, meaning *This is not a pipe*. Seemingly paradoxical, it nonetheless makes sense. Indeed, this is merely an *image* of a pipe, and the image, said Magritte, is not to be confused with the real thing.

Free Association

Imagination is related to what is called "free association," the unprescribed connecting of disparate thoughts, words, and images from different contexts. Psychologist Arthur Koestler has pointed out that "in humor, both the *creation* of a subtle joke and the *re-creative* act of perceiving the joke involve the delightful mental jolt of a sudden leap from one plane or associative context to another."[6] Psychologist Silvano Arieti reminds us that one of the mainstays of human cognition is the brain's ability to make associations, regardless of how far-fetched they may seem to be. The person who sees a similarity between a logical statement and an irrational one, and makes the listener or viewer momentarily believe that this similarity is an actual identity, creates a witticism or joke.[7]

Shimomura's paintings reflect his fascination for comparing American culture with that of Japan. He juxtaposes Utamaro's beauties with Minnie Mouse, and ukio-ye figures with Disney cartoon characters. "I have become a dispassionate viewer of my own layering system," says the artist. "After years of concern about content, I feel no longer compelled to project my own point of view towards the things that concern me. Rather, I find myself more interested in creating a visual forum that expresses ironic and contradictory attitudes towards these concerns."

Roger Shimomura, *Untitled (Donald Duck)*, 1986. Oil on canvas, 31" x 31" (79 x 79 cm). Greg Kucera Gallery, Seattle.

The world of reality, says yet another psychologist, William Fry, Jr., is composed of facts, units, measurements, revealed truths, numbers, principles, molecules, and evident substances. Reality is characterized as immutable, concrete, inflexible, thoroughly reliable, and predictable. Conversely, the world of fantasy is spectral, enigmatic, and subjective. It is the realm of the irrational and the absurd—a dominion of fiction, daydream, reverie, impossibility, and illusion.[8]

Through the mitigating factor of the imagination, the two worlds of reality and fantasy are merged into a *super-reality*, a realm of awakened cognition and expression. Free association helps us "shift gears" into a flexible, nonjudgmental mode of thinking. The brain is unchained from conditioned response and is free to discover new analogies by making seemingly irrational associations.

Patti Warashina's *Iron Siren* is a funny, surreal, yet poignant visual metaphor. With the subject of women's issues in mind, the artist's free association may have transpired as follows:

Often [wit] has been studied as a form of art; at times as a psychological process; occasionally as a special expression of the spirituality of man.
Silvano Arieti, 20th-century American writer and psychologist

9

Iron > a home appliance associated with "woman's work" > iron alludes to bond, chain, shackle > iron-willed connotes determined, resolute, set > sound-alike word, "siren" > alluring, bewitching, enchanting mythological female; also alarm sound signifying emergency > irony denotes "incongruity between situation and expectation," thereby punning on the words iron/irony = A visual idea from the word combination "iron siren" : A three-dimensional image of a stereotypical housewife liberated from the kitchen and laundry room, into an iron-willed siren who has transformed the iron-shackle into an escape craft to set sail for a new horizon?[9]

Exactly *how* the mind works to produce a creative idea is still a mystery, even to its producer. Because of the subjective element in humor, artists sometimes have difficulty responding to questions such as, "What makes your art funny?" or "Where do your ideas come from?" Generally, we know that creativity arises from the interplay between the unconscious and conscious mind. Although there is little information about how the unconscious mind processes the information presented to it,

With punnery and satire, the artist draws attention to gender issues.
Patti Warashina, *Iron Siren*, 1979. Clay and glaze, wood, plastic base, 25" x 20" x 20" (63.5 x 50.8 x 50.8 cm). Courtesy of the Bentley Gallery, Scottsdale, Arizona.

we do know that free association—the mental play that accepts seemingly ambiguous information—kindles creativity.

For free association to take place, some preliminary work must be done so that the brain will have a variety of data to manipulate playfully and transform. Whether in fine or popular art, the visual humorist must keep informed of social and political issues and be a keen observer of humanity in action. The parodist, satirist, and caricaturist perceives the "hot issues" of the day and brainstorms selected subjects to convert into visual ideas. This is how cartoonist Mort Gerberg describes his search for ideas: "Once I have some starting subjects in my head, my brain becomes like an old telephone switchboard, where wires are plugged into holes and a light goes on when a connection is made. So I let my mind 'doodle' different combinations of words on my notebook pages until I make a connection."[10]

Making the Ordinary Strange

Picasso once said, "It's not in the way you look at your subject that is important, but the way you see it." The first question we should ask, then, is: How can we learn to see differently, creatively?

Henri Poincaré hypothesized that creative thought emerges from the unconscious as a result of *incubation*. After we do preliminary work on a problem, we take a short break to allow the unconscious, in its mysterious ways, to "cook" the subject. To make the ordinary strange, and to create humor, one needs to disengage, let the conscious mind rest, and allow a period of gestation.[11]

Interestingly, the unconscious usually presents its insights during moments of reverie, when one isn't thinking of anything in particular, such as during a quiet walk, a long drive, or while shaving or showering, or engaging in other automatic activities.

Incubation, intuition, or unconscious scanning come into play

Gilbert's whimsical sculpture is a tribute to the "self-made man," the entrepreneur who has lifted himself up by his bootstraps, wired his own brain, and graduated with honors from the school of hard knocks.

John Martin Gilbert, *Self-Made Man*, 1980. Mixed media, 12" x 7" x 5" (30.5 x 17.8 x 12.7 cm). Courtesy of the artist.

Sewell's constructions are made up of un-
likely art materials: junk, skillfully assembled.
He is a bricoleur, the kind of artist who turns
trash into treasure. He calls his local navy
dump "a gold mine."

Leo Sewell, *Seated Lady*. Found objects, 51"
x 20" x 3" (129.5 x 50.8 x 83.8 cm). Courtesy of the artist.

when we are creative. Unconscious scanning, a process Anton Ehren-
zweig has described, can handle information that is fuzzy, incomplete,
or incoherent to the rational faculties. The interplay between this scanning and conscious differentiation allows us to surface the "hidden order of the unconscious."

The Play Principle

Creative individuals recognize the importance of play and its relationship to wit, humor, and art. Making comic situations is not unlike children's play insofar as it is an excursion in fantasy and make-believe.
Playfulness in art, however, is not simply an evasion of reality, but
rather, as Silvano Arieti puts it, "a substitution of a bit of creativity for
what it replaces or temporarily suspends from the focus of consciousness."[12]

"The play principle calls forth intuition," writes Steven Heller. "Intuition is a switch that starts and stops the play process, controlling when
the artist will move from childlike abandon into adult-like premedita-
tion."[13] Without a doubt a part of the adventure of art lies in creative
play. As Ralph Waldo Emerson so poignantly stated, "It is a happy talent
to know how to play."

Humor-Triggering Mechanisms

The objective world is not intrinsically funny but somehow *made* funny
by the humorist. To create visual humor, consciously or unconsciously,
the artist employs certain psychological "mechanisms" that transform a
subject by transposing it into a surprisingly different context. For the
purposes of study, and fun, we can dub the part of the brain that takes
ordinary things and makes them amusing "the humorizer," and call its
tools "humor-triggering mechanisms."

Starting on page 14 are eleven humor-triggering mechanisms
(HTMs) that can be used by your humorizor to initiate free association
and inspired analogical disorder.

Prescott's amusing kinetic sculpture bids the viewer to "please touch." It is a miniature environment, a parody and caricature of American life made all the more entertaining by the artist's use of bright, funky colors and shapes, and bizarre movement set into motion by touch.

Fredrick Prescott, *Galaxy Drive-in*, 1996. Metal, color, neon, 34" x 23" x 10" (86.4 x 58.4 x 25.4 cm). Courtesy of the artist.

Picasso's substitution of a toy automobile for the baboon's head affords an ingenious visual pun.

Pablo Picasso, *Baboon and Young*, 1951. Bronze, 21" x 13¼" x 6⅞" (53.3 x 33.7 x 17.5 cm). Museum of Modern Art, New York, Mrs. Simon Guggenheim Fund.

Association Combining, juxtaposing, free associating, connecting, comparing, superimposing, coalescing. Uniting anomalous elements from different physical or psychological realms. Making stretched analogies and associations that produce surprise and incongruity. Hybridizing. Producing "unique crossbreeds" by mating disparate elements.

Transposition Shifting, transferring, switching, exchanging, adapting, substituting, replacing, displacing, relocating. Transferring a subject into a new context or situation, into a different time or gender; moving a subject out of its normal placement; changing historical, social, geographical, or political settings.

Transformation Changing, evolving, progressing, transmutating, metamorphosing, hybridizing. Altering composition, structure, form, character, condition, or appearance of a subject. Stylizing, abstracting, transfiguring an image or form by caricature, exaggeration, or distortion.

Contradiction Reversing, twisting things around, producing incongruity, ambiguity, paradox, irony, displaced logic, double-entendre, mixed metaphor. Representing through the opposite.

Exaggeration Overstating or understating, hyperbole, embellishing "truth," distorting, caricaturing, prevaricating. Exaggerating to ridiculous extreme, bombast. Magnifying or diminishing an object, idea, or situation; tomfoolery, jocularity.

Parody Mimicking, burlesquing, spoofing, comic representation, "roasting," or lampooning. Making comic or mildly satiric references to human behavior, customs, conventions, beliefs, or creations.

Punning Word play, word/image play, comic ambiguity, double meaning. Creating humor with ambiguity or double-entendre. Use of silly titles, malapropisms, spoonerisms, alterations of the expected.

Disguise Concealing, deceiving, camouflaging, obscuring, obfuscating. Hiding or encrypting certain elements. Masking, making something ambiguous. Use of personal (or cryptic) symbolism or metaphor, double or multiple meaning, or subliminal information.

Satire Ridiculing, mocking, applying trenchant wit, irony, or sarcasm to tweak the conscience, or trigger awareness. Poking fun at human hypocrisy, vice, and folly. Iconoclasm, deriding "sacred cows."

A corner grocery store in the form of a milk container? Anything that can be imagined can be made "real" in art. Free association, *transposition (dislocation), exaggeration,* and *contradiction* create this comic fantasy.

Mark Farand, *Jersey and Holstein*, 1994. Watercolor. Courtesy of the artist.

Whimsy, transposition, contradiction, and *exaggeration* are humor-triggering mechanisms evident in this ceramic sculpture.

Peter Vanderberge, *Animalman*, 1989. Ceramic. Courtesy of the John Natsoulas Gallery.

Targeting imperfection and malpractice in social and political groups and organizations. Criticizing ethical, moral, spiritual apathy, and corruption.

Narration Storytelling, myth making, discourse by words and/or images; graphic presentation of actions or events; sequenced graphic representation (for example, narration in a comic-strip format).

Appropriation "Borrowing," taking, annexing, conscripting, quoting, referring. Creating new work by adapting an image from a previously known art form, or from other realms of human expression. Transforming or reinventing an appropriated subject by redrawing or restyling it, or by setting it into a new context.

Why Visual Humor?

Typically, artists are motivated to create visual humor for the following reasons: *entertainment, information, and advocacy.*

As entertainment, visual humor provides momentary escape from the world's trials and offers pleasant diversion.

Because visual humor informs largely through pictorial information, it is generally, if not sometimes universally, understood and appreciated. Iconography—the use of pictures as a language of communication—shows us the life and times, and the environment and society of an artist. Artists use iconography for visual narrative; to relate significant issues and events of their lives, their concerns, beliefs, and superstitions; and to tell of adventures of commoners, heroes, villains, and fools.

Artists with advocacy in mind communicate an overt or covert message, a message that is issued with the expectation that the viewer will support a cause, buy a product, or change an opinion.

In the chapters that follow, we'll briefly survey the history of visual humor and how artists have employed humorous visual iconography at different times and in different cultures. Also, you'll see how artists entertain, inform, and advocate through a wide variety of visual genres.

Sean Read is a contemporary British artist who presents a wry and farcical account of artist-client commerce. The image is funny, yet parodies the aspiring artist's plight in seeking recognition.

Sean Read, *The Artist Woos His Client*, 1994. Fiberglass and acrylic, 77" x 85" x 3.9" (196 x 216 x 10 cm). Nicholas Treadwell Gallery, Bradford, England.

A Legacy of Visual Humor

We need a history of laughter as we need a history of love, of death, of fear, of failure, to illuminate the evolution of humanity.

Robert M. Polhemus, b. 1935
American author and
English professor

Chapter 2

The contemporary artist with a penchant for humor is a direct descendant of those blithe spirits of art history who've shown that one can simultaneously laugh at a situation and take it seriously—and that jokes can be told in pictures as well as words. Visual humor is probably as old as civilization itself. Yet for those bent on researching its ancient accounts, there is scant information available. Sad but true, visual humor has had a mostly unrecorded history. Aristotle was the first to lament that comedy has had no history because it was not at first treated seriously. It seems that in olden times, laughter was often thought of as a characteristic of folly and ill manners. Ecclesiastes, a book of the Old Testament, preaches the evils of humor by saying, "I said of laughter, it is mad...and of mirth, what doeth it?"

Facing Page:
Pablo Picasso, *La Joie de Vivre (The Joy of Life)*, 1946. Musee Picasso, Antibes.

Three-faced Head from a Misericord, New College, Oxford, c. 1386–1395. Dover Archives, New York.

View from the Margin

In *Comic Faith*, Robert M. Polhemus speculates that one reason for the slow rise of appreciation for comic expression is that laughter and comic revelry have been tinged with an aura of blasphemy. He explains that the heritage of Greek idealism and Judeo-Christian monotheism has taught that an active sense of humor has an unsavory quality about it, and because humor can make authority appear ludicrous, it threatens a sense of law and order.[1]

Perhaps time has amended this view. Today's psychologists concur that comic imagination is a healthy aspect of human behavior and is of vital importance to the regeneration, transformation, and sanctification of life. Nevertheless, visual humor, in some contexts, has not been taken completely seriously, and it is still perceived by some as politically dangerous.[2]

In a quasi-cartoon style, the Greek artist Sophilos depicts the wedding of Peleus and Thetis. The wine god Dionysus, shown bearing a vine is arriving as a wedding guest at the house of Peleus. He is followed by Bebe, goddess of youth, and the centaur Cheiron, who brings a practical gift of game for the wedding feast.

Sophilos, Dinos, a large wine bowl, (detail from the upper frieze), 580 BC. Ceramic, height: 28" (71 cm). British Museum.

American art critic Donald Kuspit aptly describes the nature of visual humor when he writes, "[Humorous] art today exists to preserve the possibility of 'another' interpretation of life—the possibility of a continuing view from the margin, as if not the correct one, then the correcting one, reminding us that the totality of the truth about life and art itself, is hardly in the possession of any supposed mainstream."[3] A thoughtful examination of past visual humor reveals its relation and importance to culture, its influences, as well as its inflammatory effects, and helps us better understand the conflicting attitudes toward visual humor encountered today.

An early form of caricature is revealed in this representation of animals parroting human vocations. Among the images in this historic scroll is the anthropomorphized lion and unicorn playing draughts (a form of chess); the fox playing the double flute, and the cat in charge of a drove of geese.

Two Animals Playing Draughts (scene from the Satirical Papyrus), Egyptian, c. 1185 BC, height: 3½" (9 cm). British Museum.

How Old Is Visual Humor?

The first records of the intentional use of visual humor appear to date back to the early Sumerians (c. 2000 BC) and the Egyptians (c. 1360 BC). From both of these cultures, archaeologists have discovered artifacts that show the use of parody and caricature, particularly through anthropomorphism and grotesquerie.

Among the Sumerian art unearthed in Ur (present-day Iraq) is a four-

Contemporary artist Albertson pictures animals in human pursuits. "[With my cast of animal protagonists] I try to paint what life feels like in all its contradictory aspects, beauty, and tensions."

Jim Albertson, *Painting from Life*, 1995. Oil on canvas, 37" x 45" (94 x 114.3 cm). Courtesy of the John Natsoulas Gallery.

This early Sumerian image is from the front of a large lyre.

Shell Plaque, c. 2685 BC. Shell, gold, lapis lazuli, on a lyre that is 65" (165 cm). University Museum, University of Pennsylvania, Philadelphia.

part shell plaque decoration on a lyre, c. 2650–2550 BC. A figure in the form of a "scorpion-man" and a gazelle are depicted in the task of brewing beer. Ancient Egyptian artisans primarily produced funerary art, though they appear to have made occasional diversions into the realm of humor. Possibly they were the first to picture animals in social parodies. Anthropomorphism—the portrayal of animals or human-beasts that mimic human behavior—was a popular graphic device as seen in the *Egyptian Papyrus of the Dead*, a parchment that dates back to 1000 BC.

Anthropomorphic figuration is also noted in early Greek, Assyrian, Chinese, Japanese, Hindu, and Mongolian art, most of which also deals with the pictorialization of fables and myths. The popular Hindu deity Ganesha, for example, a frequent characterization in twelfth-century carvings, is a portly and good-natured elephant. *Konsensei,* or *Gama-Rennin,* a holy man in early Japanese mythology, is associated with longevity and is portrayed as a person who can turn into a snake—the symbol of renewal.

Creature from a Han Dynasty Chariot. China. Dover Archives, New York.

Ancient Greek myths abound with acts of bravery against grotesque monsters, such as *gorgons* (snake-haired women who turn anyone who looks at them into stone), *sirens* (winged female creatures who lure sailors to their deaths with bewitching song), *sphinxes* (mysterious beings with the face of a woman, the body of a lion, and the wings of a bird), the *hydra* (a huge serpent with nine heads), *Cerberus* (the monstrous three-headed dog who guards the entry to the underworld), and *chimaera* (lionlike, fire-breathing creatures with a goat head on their back and a serpent for a tail). The world of Greek mythology is also rife with satyrs and pans—mischievous male demigods of half-human, half-beast origin.

Aside from illustrating myths and pre-Christian legends, the Greek artisan parodied earthly society by making humorous drawings on pottery and ornamental artworks. Comic satire and burlesque was rarely seen in the "high art" of Greek sculpture, but was widely

Da Vinci's caricatures grew out of studying people who were striking in appearance. He considered homeliness "a variation of beauty" and produced many of his caricatures from his memory of the people he observed in the streets.

Leonardo da Vinci, *A Group of Five Grotesque Heads*, c. 1490. Pen and ink over red chalk. Royal Library, Windsor Castle. © Her Majesty Queen Elizabeth II.

Although an object of reverence, the *Dancing Ganesha* is not without humorous overtones.

Dancing Ganesha, Malwa (Madhya Pradesh), Parama period (c. 800–1250). Sandstone, 39" (99 cm). Nelson-Atkins Museum, Kansas City, Missouri.

One laugh is worth a thousand groans.

Confucius, 551–479 BC

Chinese philosopher

represented in Greek popular crafts, where an abundance of dwarfs, beggars, hunchbacks, and drunken human figures are painted on vases and pottery. There was a search for ideal ugliness as well as ideal beauty.

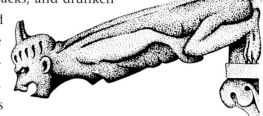

The term *grotesque* has had many different connotations throughout history. It is used to describe bizarre representations, such as *gargoyles,* which were carvings of frightening demons, traditionally used as gutter spouts on medieval buildings. Grotesque also describes eccentric behavior, "low" comedy and burlesque, early caricature, and certain expressions from Dada and Surrealist art.

Later European Grotesqueries

Oddities from the Middle Ages include *drolleries,* comic or clownish figures drawn on illuminated manuscript borders, and the *Bayeux Tapestry* (created between 1066 and 1077), a gigantic embroidery that measures 20 inches wide by 230 feet long. With bright colors and caricatured figures, the tapestry portrays the Norman invasion of Harold's England by William the Conqueror in sequenced images not unlike the present-day comic strip format. Also from the Gothic age are misericords, odd-looking figures and vignettes carved on the hinged seats of church furniture.

Leonardo da Vinci's sketchbooks include drawings of bizarre Rube Goldberg-like inventions that range from preposterous weapons of war

Above:
Lucifer and Demons (manuscript illustration), 1400s. Location unknown. Dover Publications, New York.

Above, right:
Gargoyle, European. Location unknown. Dover Publications, New York.

to ingenious, though improbable, flying machines. Comic grotesqueries appear in the work of Jacques Callot (1592–1635), a French engraver who worked in Rome and, inspired by the Italian *commedia dell'arte,* produced bizarre caricatures of beggars and individuals with deformities. Caricatures of pygmies and dwarfs in combative sporting events were also portrayed by the Italian engraver Stefano Della Bella (1610–1664), mainly as entertainment for the Grand Duke of Tuscany.

In Northern Europe, the image of the satyr resurfaces in the work of Albrecht Dürer and his followers in the early 1500s. Dürer's satyr, as seen in his engraving *Satyr's Family with Ornament* (page 26), is not a lecherous goat-man as depicted in Greek mythology but a "noble man-beast" dedicated to the protection of women and children.

Into the Western Modern Ages

The invention of printing in the fifteenth century allowed the art of graphic satire to be produced and circulated in large numbers. Unlike art that was destined for display, early prints were studied in private and concealed from those who would not approve of their content. Edward

The image of the Satyr, popular in early Greek art, emerges again in the work by Dürer in the 1500s. However, instead of the ribald and lusty character of Greek origin, Dürer depicts the Satyr as a noble savage who defends family values and protects women and children from harm.

Albrecht Dürer, *Satyr's Family with Ornament*, (detail) 1505. Woodcut, Metropolitan Museum of Art, New York.

Lucie-Smith states in *The Art of Caricature*, "For the first time art was free to comment without inhibition on topical themes."[4]

From the printing press came broadsheets, weekly and daily circulars and newspapers featuring political and social commentary, and the political cartoon. The broadsheet shifted from the presentation of religious motifs and themes of the devil as the source of moral ills to pictorial narration of topical stories of love and war. William Hogarth (1697–1764), who favored including engraved picture stories in a portfolio of prints to be viewed in sequential order, elevated the broadsheet to an art form.

Generally speaking, humor and art, particularly in the art of Europe and from the Renaissance to the early twentieth century, have been relegated to separate domains. British critic Roger Malbert describes the humor-impoverished art world in these terms: "Rarely has the comic vision been allowed to disturb the sanctity of the painter's studio. The greatest exceptions such as Bruegel, Hogarth, Goya and Daumier, were also supreme printmakers, and until the era of mass reproduction, it was the print that proved the most efficient vehicle for pictorial social com-

bye teylten fy auß oye facramēt fchick
ten zwen partickel gen Prag. zwē gen
falczpurg.zwen yn oie Newenftat

bye verprenten fy oie facramēt verfu=
chen ob vnfer glaub gerecht wer flogē
auß dem offen zwen engel.vñ.ij.taubē

Although many of the early broadsheets had a comic strip-like format, their narrative was anything but comic. Generally, their sequence narrated moral or propagandistic issues, set mainly in pictographic form and directed to a mass audience.

An example of a broadsheet (detail), published in Nuremberg, Germany in the 1490s.

ment. Only in this century...did the anarchic spirit of humor and satire enter the mainstream of high art. England still does not really value its tradition of graphic satire, despite the fact that several of the finest draughtsmen and watercolorists in the history of English art were caricaturists."[5]

The coexistence of humor and art has a history that has evolved and regenerated over time through the work of artists who take their humor seriously. Artist-humorists have used similar approaches from age to age, such as the discordant image, distorted or grotesque figuration, incongruous juxtapositions, mocking caricature, and conceptualizations of the absurd, among other "mechanisms" discussed throughout this book.

A Survey of Artists

It is impossible within the limits of this book to take account of all those who have made a significant contribution to visual humor as art. Nevertheless, here are some of the artists, from the fifteenth century to the present, who have contributed to the legacy of visual humor in both high and low art.

Hieronymus Bosch Bosch (c. 1450–1516) was a master of grotesque satire and a moralist who painted dark and satiric representations. His "grand moralities" reflect uncontrolled human passions, the fearful consequences of sin and folly, and the tortures of "the damned." Among his best-known paintings is the *Garden of Earthly Delights*, which hangs in Madrid's Prado Museum.

Two other notable satirists from this epoch are **Edhard Schöen** (1491–1542), an artist who delighted in ridiculing the German Reformation leader Martin

Facing page:
The haunting phantasmagoria and black humor depicted in Bosch's allegorical painting can rightly be described as "a sermon in visual form." Bosch's iconography centers on the vicissitudes of human existence and the consequences of sin, in a pictorial cosmos that closely parallels a lunatic asylum.

Hieronymus Bosch, *Garden of Earthly Delights* (third panel of triptych), c. 1500. 86½" x 38" (219 x 97 cm). British Museum.

Loach's message echoes that in Bosch's *Garden of Earthly Delights.* Like the legendary Faustus, modern civilization appears to have made a pact with the devil, having sacrificed spiritual values for material gains. The painting also recalls the prophetic words of writer Francis Marion Crawford: "The devil knoweth his own, and is a particular bad paymaster."

Roberta Loach, *Civilization Has Made Its Bargain with Mephistopheles*, 1993. Acrylic on canvas, 56" x 47" (142.2 x 119.4 cm). Courtesy of the artist.

Sixteenth-century caricatures frequently dealt with the religious controversy between Martin Luther's followers and Roman Catholics. In this print, the Reformation leader is a bagpipe in the service of the devil. The image of the bagpipe is also a facetious allusion to the long-winded nasal drawl of the friars of the time.

Edhard Schöen, *The Devil Playing Luther as a Pair of Bagpipes*, 1521. Woodcut with color applied. Public Domain Archives.

Above:

Bruegel's paintings are parables of human folly and are often inspired by the Gospels or ancient homilies, such as the eleventh-century English homily, *And gret fisches etes the smale. For riche men of this werd etes, that pouer wit thair travail getes.*

Pieter Bruegel the Elder, *The Big Fish Eat the Little Fish*, 1550. Pen and ink drawing. Albertina Museum, Vienna.

Left:

Bruegel presents a mocking commentary of artist–critic relations. The artist is shown as a visionary with keen hand and fixed concentration, while the "connoisseur" is depicted as a slightly befuddled and dull-witted oaf, with his hand firmly clutching his money bag.

Pieter Bruegel, *The Painter and the Connoisseur*, c. 1568. Pen and bistre (a brown pigment), 10" x 8⅜" (25.4 x 21.3 cm). Albertina Museum, Vienna.

Luther, and **Lucas Cranach** (1472–1533), a painter who lampooned the papacy.

Pieter Bruegel the Elder

Bruegel (c. 1525–1569) was a Flemish painter and satirist who followed the tradition of Bosch and drew on the same resources of fantasy and realism to expose greed and moral corruption. Many of Bruegel's works are comic-tragic scenarios that depict well-known parables. His pen and ink drawing, *The Big Fish Eat Little Fish,* is an example of the symbolic—or indirect approach—in producing social commentary. Bruegel was once nicknamed "Pieter the Droll" and thought to be a victim of a harmless form of madness (the passion for visual satire), which gets worse with age.

Giuseppe Arcimboldo

Arcimboldo (1537–1593), Milanese painter and pioneer of the visual pun, is famous for his grotesque figures composed of fruits, vegetables, and miscellaneous objects. Although his work was considered to be in poor taste in his own time, it later inspired the Surrealists of the early 1900s and continues to inspire artists today.

The Carraci Family (Annibale, Augostino, Ludovico)

In the 1590s, the Carracis—an Italian family of fine artists—created comic portrait drawings, which they dubbed *caricaturas,* meaning "loaded" portraits. Their comically exaggerated likenesses were created in the spirit of entertainment and game, rather than for social commentary.

William Hogarth

Modern political cartooning began in mid-eighteenth-century England with the etchings and paintings of engraver William Hogarth. His *Characters and Caricaturas* (see page 32) lampoon the Carraci family's drawings, which he dismissed as "trivial humor." Hogarth coined the term *caricature* and defined it to mean an art that strives to present true "character and moral truth," in opposition to the Italian "caricatura," which he considered "mere diversion." In the period between 1731 and 1745,

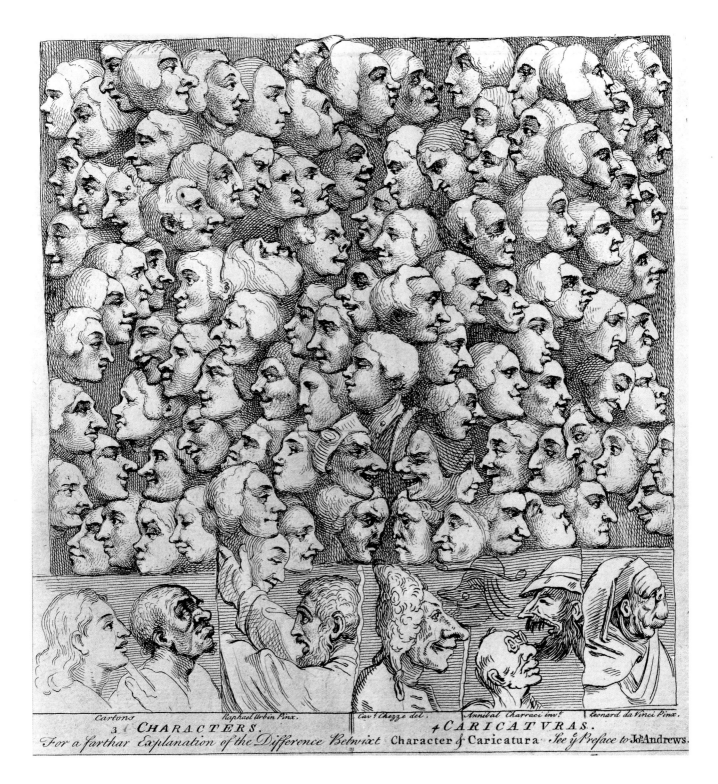

Cartons   Raphael Urbin Pinx.   Cav.ᵉ Chezze del.   Annibal Charraci inv.ᵗ   Leonard da Vinci Pinx.

3 CHARACTERS.   4 CARICATVRAS.

For a farthar Explanation of the Difference Betwixt Character & Caricatura See y.ᵉ Preface to J.ᵒ Andrews.

Hogarth produced a series of suites, each a sequence of anecdotal pictures that included *The Harlot's Progress* (six scenes), *The Rake's Progress* (eight scenes), and *Marriage a la Mode* (six scenes), each presented in a "stage-set" composition satirizing the obsessions of a decadent and corrupt society.[6] "My picture is my stage, and men and women my players," said Hogarth, paraphrasing Shakespeare.

Hogarth is considered the most important satirical printmaker of the first half of the eighteenth century and an unrivaled commentator on the manner and morals of his time.

Benjamin Franklin Franklin was the first American political cartoonist. In 1754 he drew *Unite or Die*, a cartoon that pictured the American colonies as separate pieces of a serpent, alluding to the consequences of separation. Both Franklin and Paul Revere were competent artists who drew cartoons of resistance to British tyranny.

This drawing became a potent symbol of resistance and a galvanizing force that prompted the colonists to unite against British tyranny. It was the first cartoon published in an American newspaper.

Benjamin Franklin, *Unite or Die*, 1754. The *Pennsylvania Gazette*.

James Gillray Gillray (1757–1815) is considered by many critics to be the greatest caricaturist of his time. Sardonic and remorseless in his vitriolic humor, Gillray developed a style and skill said to have raised caricature from a trade to a fine art. His pungent barbs were aimed at the royal family, government officials, the Napoleonic war, and quack doctors, among other subjects. Gillray is best remembered for his satires targeting Napoleon Bonaparte, whom he portrayed as "Little Boney." (See *The Cow-pock*, next page, and *Corsican Pest*, page 90.)

Above:
Graphic images have the power to sway public opinion. In this print Gillray ridicules a new vaccine against smallpox by showing little cows erupting from the bodies of people who have been inoculated. This scoffing notion of a valid medical practice may have deterred people from obtaining a vaccine.

James Gillray, *The Cow-pock* (or, *The Wonderful Effects of the New Inoculation*), 1802. Pen and ink, 8" x 12" (20.5 x 31 cm). British Museum.

Right:
Rowlandson was a commentator of contemporary life, a social satirist, and parodist of the reigning fads and fashions of his day. He is noted for his delicate Rococo-like drawing style and his refinement of caricature to an art form.

Thomas Rowlandson, *The Gaming Table at Devonshire House*. Metropolitan Museum of Art, New York.

Thomas Rowlandson Rowlandson (1756–1827), a British parodist and contemporary of Gillray, saw caricature as *tableau de modes*, that is, commentary on the British social scene. With a superb drawing style, he presented a rollicking and often boisterous view of the English country and city life.

George Cruikshank Cruikshank (1792–1878), a British political and social satirist, was the son of Isaac Cruikshank, also a talented caricaturist. George Cruikshank succeeded Gillray as the most popular caricaturist of his time; his subjects ranged from fashion and customs of the day to temperance and moral decadence. Although largely self-educated, Cruikshank displayed an exceptional knowledge of literature and language and eventually became an eminent political cartoonist in England. He developed a fondness for the *grand mot*—the clever witticism—which he neatly integrated in the form of text in his cartoons.

Through the centuries the caricaturist has been granted a certain immunity from censure in the same tradition accorded the Court Jester or Fool. Cruikshank, for example, was reportedly offered by the Royal Household a considerable sum of money "in consideration of a pledge not to caricature His Majesty in any immoral situation." Cruikshank dodged the sticky situation by refraining to show the licentious Prince Regent in sinful acts, but pictured him instead standing on a stool in church doing penance for his adulteries—a drawing that offered small consolation to the Regency.

Honoré Daumier

Daumier (1808–1879) was a gifted painter, sculptor, and caricaturist who added much to the art of graphic satire. His famous cartoon of Citizen King Louis-Philippe as Gargantua swallowing bags of gold extorted from the public so incensed the French government that Daumier was arrested and sent to prison for six months. As a result of his unrelenting attack on the government, in 1835 all forms of political satire were temporarily suppressed by the French government. Daumier's political prints were a dominant influence of public opinion in Europe for thirty years. He worked by the credo, "One must be of one's own time" and produced over 5000 political drawings during his career. (See page 51.)

Gustave Doré

Doré (1823–1883) was a popular French illustrator, who created grotesque images, caricatures, and fantastic compositions.

> For health and the constant enjoyment of life, give me a keen and ever present sense of humor; it's the next best thing to an abiding faith.
> George B. Cheever, 1807–1890
> American clergy and author

Gustave Doré, *Inhabitants of Gaster's Island.* Illustration for Rabelais' *Gargantua and Pantagruel*, 1854. Courtesy of Dover Publications, New York.

His bizarre representations reached their zenith in his illustrations of François Rabelais' books of Gargantua and Pantagruel, and in his pictorialization of the adventures of Baron von Münchausen.

James Ensor

A Belgian artist, Ensor (1860–1949) painted fantastic and macabre subjects in the 1880s. Dark and grotesque in nature, his bizarre compositions centered on skeletons, death, and often gruesome scenes possessed of an ironic humor reminiscent of Bosch and Bruegel. Although Ensor's black humor is chilling, it is not without comic overtones and a twisted sense of fun.

The black humor of James Ensor is an iconoclastic type of comedy, a tragic farce or "comedy of the absurd." One skeleton has a violin, another a palette, suggesting that brilliance in music and art are defunct. A third skeleton stands next to an unlit lamp, a symbol that the "Lamp of Truth" no longer shines.

James Ensor, *Skeletons Warming Themselves*, 1889. Oil on canvas, 29½" x 23⅜" (75 x 58.4 cm). Kimbell Art Museum, Fort Worth.

Busch pioneered the idea of "the comic picture story" in Europe. In this episode, the young scalawags have schemed a way of pilfering a barbecued chicken.

Wilhelm Busch, *Max and Moritz*, from the storybook, *Max und Moritz*, 1865.

Rodolphe Töpffer and Wilhelm Busch The concept of creating *time* by a chronological sequence of images (as in the comics) was pioneered by Rodolphe Töpffer and Wilhelm Busch. Töpffer, a Swiss artist and educator, devised his first picture stories in 1827. In 1865, Busch, a German book illustrator, created *Max and Moritz*, an illustrated adventure of two young pranksters. Because both artists popularized the format of "picture stories," they are acknowledged as founders of the modern-day comic strip.

Thomas Nast One of the most famous early American political cartoonists is Thomas Nast (1840–1902). Nast gained his reputation as a cartoonist for *Harper's Weekly* during the Civil War, but is best remembered for his powerful political cartoons in 1871, which skewered the corrupt William Marcy "Boss" Tweed, head of New York's infamous Tammany Hall Ring. Nast's caricatures single-handedly aided in the capture of Tweed, who had fled to Spain to escape justice. Spanish authorities recognized and apprehended the fugitive based on the caricatures. It was Thomas Nast who created the symbols of the Republican party elephant and the Democrat's donkey, still in use in American politics.

George Grosz Grosz (1893–1959), a German-American artist, objected to the German people's patriotic support of an immoral government in his acrid political and social satires. Grosz was also a leading member of the Dada group in Berlin after 1918 and later settled in New York City in 1923 to teach at the Art Students' League. He was hailed by critics as "the most powerful political satirist since Goya and Daumier."

Opposite, top:
Nast's satiric cartoons of "Boss" Tweed played a decisive role in bringing down Tweed's corrupt political machine that plundered New York City of millions of dollars.

Thomas Nast, *Who Stole the People's Money?—Do Tell*, 1871. Pen and ink. *New York Times*.

Opposite, bottom:
Grosz's abrasive humor satirizes Berlin's deteriorating postwar society of the 1920s.

George Grosz, *Café*, 1922. Pen and ink, 12⅜" x 25½" (31.5 x 64.8 cm). Museum of Modern Art, New York.

Below:
Surprising and often amusing images are perceived in dreams when the unconscious, unshackled by logic, freely associates disparate images. Ernst's surreal vision explores the realm of the unconscious, which in Ernst's words, is aimed at presenting "a psychological biography of emotional perspectives." "Super-reality"—the essence of Surrealism—is by Ernst's admission, "a function of our will to put everything completely out of place."

Max Ernst, *Capricorn*, 1947. Bronze, Staatliche Museen, Berlin. Photography by Reinhard Friedrich.

Modern Masters of Visual Humor

Lyonel Feininger   Born in New York of German-American parents, Feininger (1871–1956) was an expressionist painter, educator, filmmaker, and cartoonist who created the comically surreal strips, *Kin-Der-Kids* and *Wee Willie Winkie* (1906).

Pablo Picasso   The Spanish painter (1881–1973), who figured prominently in practically every evolutionary phase of modern art, also adopted and integrated caricature into fine art. Critic Adam Gopnik explains that it was the language of the comic strip that inspired Picasso to produce the two most important images of suffering of pre-World War II art: *Guernica* and *The Dream and Lie of Franco*, both painted in 1937. (See *La Joie de Vivre* on page 18 and *Baboon and Young* on page 14.)

Max Ernst   Ernst (1891–1976) was leader of the Cologne Dada group in 1919. His paintings, collages, and sculptures of the mid-1900s were based on the exploration of dreams and the unconscious. Ernst developed a dreamlike mythology in his work, which allied him to the school of Surrealism. Although mainly enigmatic and appealing to the subconscious for conciliation, many of his works are curious aggregates of anthropomorphized and hybridized figures and not entirely bereft of comic parody.

Marcel Duchamp   Duchamp (1887–1968), the French-American painter, Dadaist, and iconoclast, created a sensation with works such as *Nude Descending a Staircase* and his pun-laden constructions. He is the inventor of the "ready-made." *Why Not Sneeze* is a visual oxymoron and an excellent example of the artist's penchant for wit and humor. (See *Bicycle Wheel* on page 108.)

Marc Chagall   Chagall (1887–1985) was inspired by untutored folk art and the Fauve painting style. He was a joyous artist with a full devotion to romantic love. His painting *I and the Village* is a kaleidoscopic,

simultaneous representation of recollected memories presented in the artist's typical faux-naif style.

Paul Klee

Klee (1879–1940), Swiss painter and teacher, was one of the most inventive and prolific of modern artists. He mixed poetic fantasy with a comic pictorial style and communicated a childlike wonder in his visionary works. His disjunctive method of composition and his appeal to a sense of the comic and the absurd, has had a major influence on the development of modern art.

David Low

Low (1891–1963) was a British editorial cartoonist and arguably the greatest political satirist of World War II. His cartoons have been hailed as visual counterparts to the speeches of Winston Churchill.

Joan Miró

This Spanish painter (1893–1983) delved in many styles, from Cubism to Surrealism, and was often inspired by comic strips, particularly George Herriman's *Krazy Kat*.

Alexander Calder

Calder (1898–1976), American sculptor and painter, invented the mobile. He dedicated the majority of his studio output to the joy of festivity and play. His comic wire sculptures of figures and animals brought him worldwide attention and helped move humor into mainstream art.

Al Hirschfeld

Hirschfeld (b. 1903), one of the best theater caricaturists of the century, has been drawing caricatures of Broadway shows and stars for the *New York Times* since the early 1920s. (See page 44.)

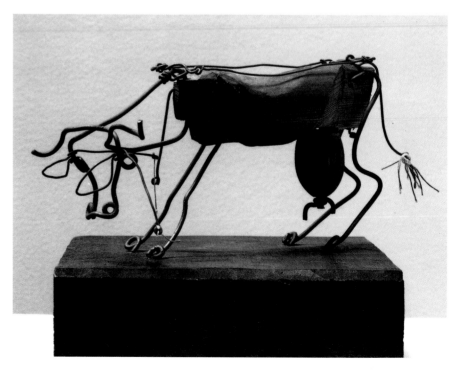

The whimsical wire caricatures of Alexander Calder are line drawings in three dimensions. Calder: "I think best in wire."

Alexander Calder, *Cow*, 1929. Wire and wood construction, 3½" on wood base 2" x 6" x 5¾" (5.2 x 15 x 14.5 cm). Museum of Modern Art, New York.

André Breton once said, "Miró is probably the most Surrealist of us all." Particularly fond of George Herriman's *Krazy Kat*, Miró said that in painting *Dog Barking at the Moon*, he was simply making "a kind of comic."

Joan Miró, *Dog Barking at the Moon*, 1926. Oil on canvas, 28⅞" x 36½" (73.3 x 92.7 cm). Philadelphia Museum of Art.

One of America's most beloved theater artists, Hirschfeld prefers to be called a "characterist" rather than a caricaturist. His work invokes no malice whatsoever. Hirschfeld has the uncanny ability to capture the likenesses of his subject with sparseness of line and excellent sense of decorative design. The artist delights in encrypting his daughter's name, Nina, into his characterizations.

Al Hirschfeld, *Carol Burnett, Jack Lemmon, Walter Matthau, Billy Wilder*, from the movie version of *The Front Page*, 1973. Courtesy of the artist.

Below:
Echoing the style of Arcimboldo, albeit in three-dimensional form, Sewell fashions amusing likenesses of animals by assembling cast-away materials collected from flea markets and junkyards.

Leo Sewell, *Boxer*, 1994. Found objects, 31" x 11" x 22" (78.7 x 27.9 x 55.9 cm). Photo: Dean Powell. Courtesy of the artist.

Herblock Herbert Block (b. 1909), the American Pulitzer prize-winning editorial cartoonist for the *Washington Post*, has had an influential and long-running career.

Saul Steinberg An American painter and cartoonist (b. 1914 in Romania), Steinberg's drawings range from parody to the absurd and irrational.

Jack Levine Levine (b. 1915) was one of the American Social Realists and a social satirist. (See *The Feast of Pure Reason* on page 93.)

Ronald Searle British graphic artist Searle (b. 1920) has created humorous drawings for magazines, such as *Punch* and *New Yorker*, and has illustrated several books.

H. C. Westermann This American sculptor (b. 1922) combines superb craftsmanship with eccentric and enigmatic humor, sometimes in obvious visual puns. (See *Object Under Pressure*, page 58 and *Evil New War God*, opposite.)

Robert Rauschenberg Rauschenberg (b. 1925) has explored collage and assemblage in addition to his paintings. His "combine paintings" of the 1950s and 1960s have had a major influence on artists

worldwide. Rauschenberg's assemblages, such as *Coca Cola Plan*, are founded on the union of disparities, an amalgamation that spontaneously presents surprising, eccentric, and often comical parodies.

Claes Oldenburg This American artist (b. 1929 in Sweden) is famous for his hyper-scaled mundane objects and soft sculptures. (See *Giant Floor Cake* on page 50.)

Jules Feiffer Feiffer (b. 1929) has a cartoon style that features monologues, dealing with modern-day psychological and sexual angst.

Marisol Escobar Escobar (b. 1930) combines assemblage, wit, and humor in her satirical sculpture.

longer seen as jokes but as mysterious, irrational visions."[7]

Red Grooms Grooms (b. 1937) is an innovator of cartoonlike happenings and site-specific installations, which mix theater, circus, comic strip, and parade.

Robert Arneson San Francisco ceramicist and influential teacher, Arneson (b. 1930) uses himself as a subject to produce sardonically witty and well-crafted sculpture. An influential teacher, he was principal founder of the Funk and figurative ceramic movement in California in the early sixties.

Gladys Nilsson, James Nutt, Karl Wirsum These three artists of the *Hairy Who*, a Chicago art group of the 1960s, spoofed urban angst, crassness, and mainstream art, using cartoon imagery and puns. They also used naive, folk, primitive, psychotic, and surreal references to develop their comically surreal styles. (See *Tilling* on page 55.)

Humor as an Art Form

Visual humor started in caricature, as social and political parody, and bounced into fine art. Since the beginning of the twentieth century, an interdependent relationship has developed between high and low art. Picasso influenced the direction of modern art by his attraction to archaic and primitive art, which inspired an expressive style closely aligned to caricature. Adam Gopnik observes, "After 1912, part of the creative logic of modern art involved taking a comic or satiric motif and using it in a new context of ideas and associations. If caricature had been born as a new way of looking at the grotesque, a vein of modern art was rooted in a new way of looking at caricature, in which distortion, stylization, and the marriage of the demonic and the near at hand were no longer seen as jokes but as mysterious, irrational visions."[7]

Left:
Facetious humor and satire typify Arneson's brand of visual humor. *California Artist* is a mocking self-portrait in response to a New York critic who wrote that the artist's work would never have serious depth or meaning due to the spiritual and cultural impoverishment in California.

Robert Arneson, *California Artist*, 1982. Glazed ceramic, 78" x 28" x 21" (198.1 x 71.1 x 53.3 cm). Collection, San Francisco Museum of Art. Courtesy of the John Natsoulas Gallery.

Above:
Lichtenstein is perhaps the preeminent pop artist to paraphrase the comic strip. He isolates frames from the comics, enlarges, stylizes, and re-composes them slightly to give them new life as reconstructed clichés.

Roy Lichtenstein, *Whaam!*, 1963. Magna on canvas, 68" x 160" (172.7 x 406.4 cm). Tate Gallery, London.

Below:
Launched in 1985, *Calvin and Hobbes* became a phenomenal success and lasted until 1995, when Waterson decided to retire the strip. True to their namesakes—theologian and reformer John Calvin and philosopher Thomas Hobbes—the protagonists Calvin, a hyperactive six year old and Hobbes, his toy tiger playmate, often speculate on profound issues such as the meaning of life and the nature of things in the universe.

Bill Watterson, *Calvin and Hobbes: Isn't It Strange?*, (4-19-92).

The Laughing Artist

Laughter gives us freedom, and freedom gives us laughter. The person who understands the comic begins to understand humanity and the struggle for freedom and happiness.

Martin Grotjahn, 1904–1990
Psychiatrist, author

Chapter 3

omic theorists do not regard the objective world as intrinsically funny, but as somehow made funny by its human observers—particularly by mirthful, laughing artists. Laughing artists present the unexpected, using surprise and incongruity. Their visual humor upsets expectations, reinvents clichés and puns, distorts myths, subverts rules and maxims, ridicules convention, and transforms human notions of earthly reality.

Outrageous thinking, daydreaming, and free association fuel their imaginations; they make the familiar strange, and the strange familiar. To the laughing artist, every subject, idea, person, place, or thing is potentially funny.

Facing page:
George Cruikshank took particular delight in lampooning the British monarchy and the British upper class. This cartoon mocks pomposity and affectation and the ludicrous extremes of fashion and manners in a drawing room at the Queen's House, which is now Buckingham Palace.

George Cruikshank, *Inconveniences of a Crowded Drawing Room*, 1818. Pen and ink, color, 8½" x 13" (21.5 x 33 cm). British Museum.

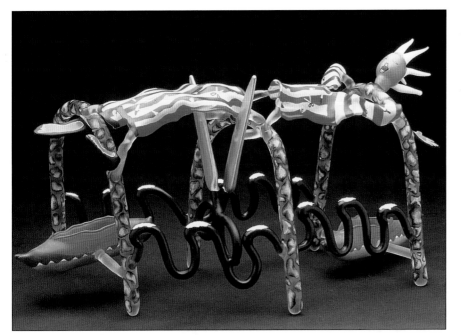

The interplay between the comically disjointed image and the title of this composition suggests that nonsense art can sometimes hide deep feelings and emotional angst.

Ginny Ruffner, *The Tunnel of Love Wears Heartbreak Pajamas*, 1989. Glass and mixed media, 13" x 26" x 14" (33 x 66 x 33.6 cm). Courtesy of the artist.

Artists Who Make the World Funny

Visual humorists tend to engage more than one mode of comic expression. In a single work, for example, an artist might blend parody and satire, or combine out-of-this-world absurdity with biting irony.

Grouping artists by mode of humor admittedly leads to oversimplification. Nevertheless, for the purpose of study I have sorted them into the following five groups, with visual examples, to provide a useful shorthand:

■ The **Whimsical Wisecracker** produces happy-go-lucky, lighthearted fun, and harmless entertainment. Creativity is expressed in the form of visual jokes and capricious imagery. Humor may vary from low-key parody to boisterous farce and burlesque. Pop Art, a movement of the 1960s, was rife with visual jokes and whimsical hyperbole. Sculptor Claes Oldenburg falls into this category, with his humorous overstatement that glorifies everyday or trivial objects.

A single gesture gains humor by means of its exaggerated expression and comic analogy to Michael Jackson's signature dance move, the "moonwalk."

Sam Hernandez, *Moonwalker,* 1988. Wood with encaustic and oil, 39" x 23" x 10" (99 x 58.4 x 25.4 cm). Courtesy of the artist.

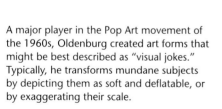

A major player in the Pop Art movement of the 1960s, Oldenburg created art forms that might be best described as "visual jokes." Typically, he transforms mundane subjects by depicting them as soft and deflatable, or by exaggerating their scale.

Claes Oldenburg, *Floor Cake (Giant Piece of Cake),* 1962. Synthetic polymer paint and latex on canvas filled with foam rubber and cardboard boxes, 58⅜" x 9' 6¼" x 58⅜" (148.2 x 290.2 x 148.2 cm). Museum of Modern Art, New York. Gift of Philip Johnson

- The **Perceptive Parodist** is a mimic who is acutely observant of reality. Parodists lampoon the customs, fads and trends, and curiosities of society and life, usually by imitating a serious subject in a ridiculous manner. Parody may range from benign satire and caricature to the burlesque.[1]

  Matt Groening ("Life in Hell," "The Simpsons"), Jules Feiffer ("Feiffer"), and Garry Trudeau ("Doonesbury") are parodists, who along with most present-day cartoonist-parodists owe much to the social and political critiques of Honoré Daumier and James Gillray, and to the more recent work of comic-strip artists Al Capp ("L'il Abner") and Walt Kelly ("Pogo," see page 53).

- **Scrappy Satirists** are hecklers who escalate the tone of humor to an aggressive pitch. Scorn and ridicule are used to vent moral outrage or to expose hypocrisy and injustice. Satirists often employ venomous caricature and mockery to skewer their subjects.

  Satire and irony are effective in Honoré Daumier's lithograph, pictured below, which shows human shortcomings with ironic overtones. Although a "kangaroo court" has clearly judged the defendant, the magistrate facetiously asks him to "speak freely" in his own defense.

> Humor wakes us up, it's a way of not taking ourselves too seriously. When things are at their worst, then you crack a joke. It's a way of getting some scale between yourself and the size of the universe.
>
> **Nick Bantock, b. 1949**
> **English-born writer**

Daumier is regarded as "godfather" of political cartooning. Combining deft and expressive drawing skill with ascerbic wit and satire, he skewered social and political hypocrisy in his time. This drawing censures a spurious judicial process.

Honoré Daumier, *You Have the Floor, What Have You to Say? Speak Freely*, 1835. Lithograph, 9⅞" x 13⅝" (251 x 346 cm). Museum of Fine Arts, Boston; bequest of William P. Babcock.

Coe: "We moved to a farm on the desert in the 1950s when I was a little girl...I remember sleeping on the screen porch on the second floor of my grandmother's house. The lizards climbing up that high would scurry over the screen and I would lie there and picture their textures in wonderful brilliant color...Like King Kong, they were special, tragic monsters. The desert might look empty on the surface but when you get in close, it is full of life. There are little plants, animals, rocks, shadows, twigs—everything is filled but the sky." (From an interview in the *Scottsdale Arizona Progress*, Dec. 18, 1981.)

Anne Coe, *Migrating Mutants*, 1986, Acrylic on canvas, 61" x 61" (154.9 x 154.9 cm). Horwitch Newman Gallery, Scottsdale, Arizona.

Many a true word is spoken in jest.

English proverb

■ The **Illuminating Ironist** confounds expectations. This humorist illuminates by antithesis—by presenting the opposite of what is expected. "Tools of the trade" for ironists are the contradictions of paradox, the clever double-entendre, and the non sequitur, in which juxtaposed visual "statements" do not follow, or together make no sense.

■ The **Artful Absurdist** takes art to the outer fringes and beyond. Nonsense humor, fantasy, and comic surrealism present a systematic outrageousness. The absurdist may draw from an eccentric imagination, exploiting the creative potential of contradiction, absurdity, and displaced logic.

The playful fantasy of Joan Miró and Max Ernst and the cryptic imagery of Marcel Duchamp, Man Ray, and René Magritte present apparent absurdities to the logic-seeking mind. Like dream images,

Walt Kelly possessed an extraordinary talent as a humorist and cartoonist. His comic strip, Pogo, is a slap-happy zoo replete with a cast of charming, wise-cracking animals. The strip features Pogo, "a possum by trade," Albert the Alligator, Deacon Muskrat, Beauregard Bugleboy, Howland Owl, and Seminole Sam. As comic-strip art it had few peers; it was beautifully drawn and had a witty and hilarious storyline. This strip made famous the ironic and often quoted line, "We have met the enemy—and he is us."

Walt Kelley, *Pogo's Earth Day*, 1971.
© O.G.P.I., used with permission.

representations by these artists seem to surface from the subconscious and appeal to subjective, nonliteral attempts at understanding. (See Chapter Five for more on these artists.)

Cartooning, discussed at the end of this chapter, is like other art genres insofar as it often crosses over or blends different kinds of humor. Depending on the idea at hand, cartoonists—especially comic-strip artists—may opt to be any combination of wisecracker, parodist, satirist, ironist, and absurdist. Cartoonists by and large have poetic license to derive ideas from life situations. The cartoon may comment on, parody, or satirize culture and its institutions, and can instruct and entertain simultaneously.

Where Visual Humor Comes From

Throughout art history, the events of everyday life have given laughing artists their inspiration and material. Whether Bosch or Daumier, Charles Schulz or Lynn Johnston, artists acquire material for art by observing the world around them. Whether painters or craftspersons, illustrators or cartoonists, creative artists are by nature acutely perceptive individuals.

Today's laughing artists read newspaper and magazine articles, watch TV news, converse, go to public events and performances, and develop their own philosophy about contemporary issues. Yet creative people

Johnson adroitly transforms Jan Vermeer's painting, *The Artist in His Studio* (1665). Johnson substitutes a female weight trainer for the figure of the woman representing the Muse of History in the Vermeer classic.

Guy Johnson,*Vermeer with Model,* 1986. Oil on paper on aluminum, 27½" x 19¾" (69.8 x 50.2 cm). Louis K. Meisel Gallery, New York.

learn to look inside themselves as well. Artists observe the everyday life of their internal world. They trust their instincts and explore their own process of creativity. What ancient Chinese philosopher Lao-tse said to his pupils about spiritual discipline might also apply to finding sources of artistic inspiration: "There is no need to run outside for better seeing...Rather abide at the center of your being; for the more you leave it, the less you learn."

Looking "inside" through self-portraiture has been one way artists have both amused and inspired themselves. Picasso made himself the subject of self-deprecating humor throughout his career, often portraying himself as a mischievous satyr or as a reluctantly aging artist. California artist Robert Arneson has also used the self-portrait for both personal and social commentary. (See *California Artist* on page 46.)

Artists generally agree that ideas come in two ways, either through a sudden flash of illumination that seems to come from nowhere, or

Left:
Gladys Nilsson is a founding member of the *Hairy Who*, a 1960s group of Chicago-based artists who initiated a funky, cartoonlike style that came to be known as Chicago Imagism. Nilsson, like other members of the group, is inspired by self-taught and naive artists, the comics, and advertising art.

Gladys Nilsson, *Tilling*, 1993. Watercolor on paper, 22" x 15" (55.9 x 38.1 cm). Courtesy of the John Natsoulas Gallery.

Above:
Arneson, who creates clay sculpture, presents a humorous portrait of himself as "kiln man."

Robert Arneson, *Kiln Man*. Ceramic. Courtesy of the John Natsoulas Gallery.

through an applied methodology. More likely than not, ideas are born of *both* methods. Just about anything can work as inspiration. Verbal language, for example, has made its way into visual language, particularly in contemporary art, not only in titles but with words, puns, clichés, and aphorisms as part of the images themselves. From Paul Klee's *Twittering Machine*, 1922 (see page 41), to the comic nonsense of Arakawa, Edward Ruscha, and beyond, the interplay between words and images has appealed to many artists and has provided a rich source for visual wit and humor.

Puns and Clichés

Zucca's clock is a miniature replica of the building that houses the New York Stock Exchange. It tells time in four locations—Bonn, Tokyo, London, and New York—the world's four financial capitals—and has a Las Vegas-style slot machine pull-handle, spinning fruit tumblers, and coins in the slot's return. This designer is said to be an inventor of a new artistic hybrid—satirical furniture-art.

Ed Zucca, *Stock Exchange Clock*, 1992. Wood, paint, currency, etc. 28" x 31" x 8½" (71.1 x 78.7 x 21.6 cm). Peter Joseph Gallery, New York.

The pun—mislabeled as the "lowest form of humor"—is a witty form of intellectual play and a wonderful igniter of unexpected imagery. Puns can be simple and direct, or sly and sophisticated.

Throughout history puns have inspired literature, poetry, and art—William Shakespeare and Marcel Duchamp are notable punsters. Duchamp's biographer, Arturo Schwarz, offers an insight as to the seemingly perpetual acceptance of the pun: "Puns, like poetry, undermine the basic supposition of a static and immutable reality: They are concerned with the equating of two different realities and the wider the gap between these two realities, the brighter will be the spark that illuminates their formerly undiscovered relationship."[2]

Among the first of the visual punsters was the sixteenth-century artist Giuseppe Arcimboldo. He painted human heads composed of fruits and vegetables (see page 31). Arcimboldo's odd-looking portraits are humorous because the images are ambiguous. Each is, at once, a still-life arrangement of fruits or vegetables and at the same time an image of a human face.

Marcel Duchamp has been described as "the most intelligent yet troublesome artist" of the first part of the twentieth century. Among Duchamp's artistic innovations was his amusing "ready-made" or found art, such as *Fountain* (1917), which was a commercially produced urinal. This object was signed and labeled by the artist and thereby proclaimed "art." According to Richard Mutt (Duchamp's tongue-in-cheek alias), it's

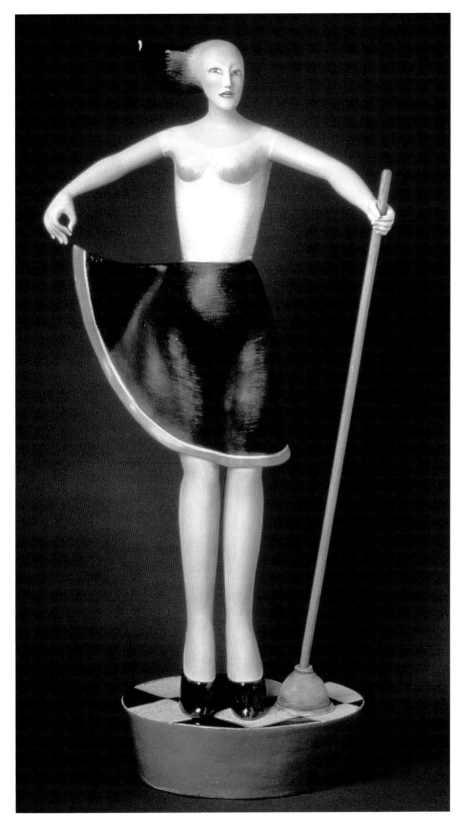

Warashina's work addresses women's issues with biting humor by drawing reference to Duchamp's ready-made *Fountain* (*Porcelain Urinal*, 1917).

Patti Warashina, *Servicing Duchamp's Porcelain*, 1993. Clay, glaze, wood, 45" x 21" x 13" (114.3 x 53.3 x 33 cm). Bentley Gallery, Scottsdale, Arizona.

Laughter is the shortest distance between two people.

Victor Borge, 20th-century Danish-born musician and humorist

not important that artists make objects with their own hands, but that they choose the object. Duchamp took an ordinary object out of its normal context and displayed it in such a manner that the original, utilitarian meaning disappeared under the new title and the new context. See his *Bicycle Wheel,* on page 108.

Besides Duchamp, many artists of the twentieth century have used puns. In the works of Chicago imagists and the California artists of the 1960s and 1970s, such as H. C. Westermann, Gladys Nilsson, Jim Nutt, Karl Wirsum, and William T. Wiley, malapropisms, misspellings, silly titles, and false nomenclature figure prominently. H. C. Westermann's *Object Under Pressure,* 1960, is both a pun and metaphor.

Clichés are another source of inspiration for the visual humorist. A *cliché* is a word, phrase, object, or idea that has become trite and stereotypical from repetitive use. A visual cliché, as distinguished from a literary one, is an image, logo, or symbol that has become hackneyed from overexposure. When flags, street signs, logos, or icons from "real life" are reinvented in a visual way, they can be transformed into something witty or intriguingly fresh.

Cartoonists use the reinvented cliché. Comic artist Mort Gerberg describes the reconstructed cliché as a trap set by the cartoonist. "The cartoonist first attracts the viewer's attention with the familiar, then fools him by changing it just enough to make it a surprise—and funny."[3]

Laughing Artists at Work

The genre of visual humor has slowly but steadily grown into an art form that is now prevalent in all modes of artistic expression. The work of visual humorists is seen in fine art, commercial art, advertising, applied art, crafts design, newspaper and magazine illustration, cinematography, cartooning, and animation.

Westermann's bizarre sculpture elicits a humorous response because of its odd combination of contradictory elements and its oblique reference to human angst and tension. "The subject matter that my work assumes is irrelevant and is only a prop upon which to hang feelings and emotions."

H. C. Westermann, *Object Under Pressure,* 1960. Wood, metal, glass, industrial gauge, 71" x 30" x 30" (180.3 x 76.2 x 76.2 cm). George Adams Gallery, New York. Photo: Nathan Rabin.

The Laughing Fine Artist

Charles Baudelaire, the French poet and critic, thought of visual humor, particularly caricature, as the *argot plastique*: "The plastic slang of civilized life and of the city is possessed of a quicksilver intelligence and mysterious double nature that allows it to capture the perplexing ambiguities of modern life in a way that stilted formal language of academic art cannot."[4]

Picasso elevated caricature to the status of fine art. Joan Miró's *Dog Barking at the Moon* (see page 43) and Constantin Brancusi's *The Kiss* are other examples of whimsical images produced in the Modernist period of the early twentieth century.

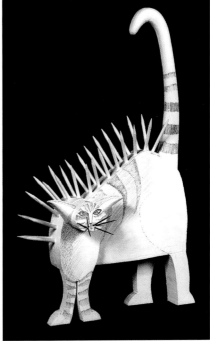

Above:
The artist's love for furry felines is evident in this whimsical portrayal—an amusing characterization of an assertive, beady-eyed, ready-for-anything, and proud-to-be-streetwise cat.

Pat Renick, *Radical Cat*, 1992. Gesso-covered styrofoam, ink and wood, 28¼" x 17½" x 3" (71.7 x 44.4 x 7.6 cm).

Left:
The artist "makes the familiar strange" by combining Leonardo's famous *Mona Lisa* with an abstract design. *Appropriation, transposition,* and *association* are mechanisms that produce the amusing incongruity.

Bernard LeDuc, *Mona Lisa*, 1994. Acrylic on cardboard, 8" x 10" (20.3 x 25.4 cm). Courtesy of the artist.

In the 1960s, two artists of note, Niki De Saint Phalle and Marisol (Marisol Escobar), reveled in the use of humor. Saint Phalle created large exuberant sculptures recalling, though not necessarily influenced by, "naive" art. Marisol's work often makes a biting comment on identity and gender issues.

Within the fine arts, humorous expression is also found in alternative or nontraditional genres. Other than painting and sculpture, or graphics and mixed media, humor comes into play in happenings, conceptual art, earthworks, installation art, and performance art.

Happenings

Red Grooms, Claes Oldenburg, and Allan Kaprow were among the first artists of the 1960s to produce the multimedia events that became known as happenings. Kaprow described happenings as environmental artworks "activated by performers and viewers."

Conceptual Art

Conceptual art evolved in the 1960s and is based on the articulation of ideas rather than actual art materials. Some conceptual art has no physical qualities at all. Photographs, maps, diagrams, and videos are used as vehicles for expression. Sol Lewitt, Bruce Nauman, Eva Hesse, and Don Celender are some of the artists who have expressed their ideas in this genre.

Installation Art

Site-specific arrangements of objects or visual effects in an indoor or outdoor space, or in a museum or gallery, comprise installations. The artist works in response to the space and according to a concept or theme. Numerous artists from the 1970s to the present have expressed their ideas through this genre, including Terry Allen, Alexis Smith, Ann Hamilton, and Sol Lewitt. Red Groom's hilarious construction, *Ruckus Manhattan*, is an early version of installation art.

Performance Art

In the late 1970s, performance art emerged as a powerful contemporary art genre. Artists performed before live audiences, using combinations of music, dance, poetry, theater, and video, in addition to visual art and print media. Performance artists Carolee Schneemann, General Idea (Canada), Gilbert and George, and Laurie Anderson were important innovators.

Earthworks Using the earth as the means for "sculpting" art evolved in the 1960s. The artistic potential of moving masses of earth, rubble, and waste materials with heavy machinery was exploited by Robert Smithson. He created *Spiral Jetty* (1970), a spiral road running into the Great Salt Lake, Utah. Walter DeMaria exhibited a room filled with dirt in a German gallery in 1968. Since then, many artists have created "environmental" works that may or may not alter landforms or water at the art site.

The artist describes this work as a satirical "dig" at tourists who travel to the Southwest primarily to shop and "take it home." The ironical image shows a pueblo on wheels.

Robert Haozous, *Portable Pueblo*, 1988. Steel, 94" x 78" x 57" (238.8 x 198.1 x 144.8 cm). Joslyn Art Museum, Omaha, Nebraska.

With a lively, eclectic imagination drawn from childhood memories, Matia conjures ideas for art furniture. This fully functional cabinet was inspired by recollections of monster movies and the legend of the famous vampire from hell. Front legs of bleached maple are the monster's fangs, the back legs of ebony are his cloak, and the upright front shelves simulate a coffin. Like the comic vampires of Charles Addams, Matia's *Dracula* is laughable in its preposterous attempt to be scary.

Alphonse Matia, *Dracula's Cabinet*, 1993. Ebony, satinwood, maple, 78" x 56" x 20" (198 x 142.2 x 50.8 cm). Peter Joseph Gallery, New York.

The Laughing Craftsperson

For centuries, the tradition of visual humor has been companion to the artist who flirts with the thin line that separates form from function. In the past decade, some of the most compelling visual humor is the work of designers, who are shaping aesthetic objects of wood, clay, fabric, glass, and mixed media. Because the boundaries that, until recently, separated fine art and popular art or craft are essentially eliminated, the craftsperson has gained recognition and respect by the international community of the avant-garde.

Art furniture and other contemporary crafts may be whimsical, but they may also carry a metaphor or vivid political message. "Ordinary furniture or applied art is inherently conservative," explains New

York gallery owner Peter Joseph, "because it is designed and manufactured to reflect the times rather than to comment on them. Contemporary art furniture, on the other hand, is intentionally provocative. It creates metaphors for its users and compels them to reflect on deeply ingrained, often unconscious, habits of seeing and use."

The mission of the artist-craftsperson is to traverse the gulf that separates art from craft. Art furniture, for example, is a more intimate art because it offers aesthetic and physical comfort in one's home on a day-to-day basis rather than on a random basis, or in the public environment of the museum.

By what means is furniture and other craft design made funny? Consciously or not, craftspersons apply their own brand of humor-triggering mechanisms. Wendell Castle, a leader in the studio-furniture movement, does it this way: "I ask myself, What if...? What if I took away this or added that? What if I turned it upside down, or if I did something crazy to it?"

Castle's *Mercury's Dream* is a fine example of the fusion of craft, art, and humor. It makes us laugh because it is a finely crafted timepiece, an outrageous neofuturistic art form, and a pun on the expression, "Time flies."

Above, right:
Dailey's lamps are noteworthy examples of consummate craftsmanship and the synthesis of form, function, and fun.

Dan Dailey, *Huntress* (Lamp), 1993. Patinated and gold-plated bronze, handblown globes, 34" x 24" x 15" (86.4 x 61 x 38 cm). Renick Gallery, Smithsonian Institution, Washington, DC.

Right:
Wendell Castle has spent the last thirty years making tables and chairs that look more like art than furniture. His creations are not only utilitarian but contemplative. The messenger god Mercury in this work appears to be moving. "My long-term goal," says Castle, "is to have furniture and art become one and the same; to have that border or division erased."

Wendell Castle, *Mercury's Dream*, 1989. Painted mahogany, cast aluminum, curly sycamore, pear, maple, electric movement, 61" x 48" x 15" (155 x 122 x 38 cm). Peter Joseph Gallery, New York.

The Laughing Illustrator

Art directors, advertisers, and illustrators all know the value of humor in the world of commerce and fully appreciate its potential to stimulate sales through advertising and promotion. They know that humorous art induces "soft sell" by providing pleasant entertainment. Humorous art is also valued by the merchandiser because it is a language that is universally understood in a society of mixed cultures.

Illustrators are not solely commissioned for advertising. Many do editorial work; that is, they create images intended for use as illustrations for book and magazine covers, textbook illustration, CD-ROM clip designs, greeting card design, T-shirt, clothing, and accessories design.

A digital image built from three negatives (turtle, church altar, and mission door). The images were processed with Adobe Photoshop software.

Dan Burkholder, *Turtle in Church, Alice, Texas*, 1993. Platinum/palladium print, 12" x 18" (30.5 x 45.7 cm). © Dan Burkholder.

The Laughing Photographer

The alert photographer can find humor in virtually every nook of the environment. City streets, parks, shopping malls, beaches, buildings, and places where people congregate—as well as marks and graffiti on buildings and walls, signs, and derelict objects—are all potential sources for discovering subjects for humorous photography. Because even the most trivial or mundane subject has potential symbolic or metaphoric value, there is latent meaning and humor in practically everything—it all depends on *how* the photographer sees and *interprets* the subject.

Straight Versus Manipulated Photography

The straight photograph records the subject as the camera lens sees it, whereas in manipulated photography, the artist *alters* what the camera records. In

This manipulated photograph is from a series that explores the mask as a metaphor for the "perfected" female, spoofing the woman who plays numerous stereotypical roles in compliance with social expectations. Magazine ads and special features, says the artist, fuel the myth by sensationalizing make-overs that promise a "new and different—and more desirable "you" through hairstyling and professional makeup.

Judith Golden, *Rhinestones (from Magazine Makeover Series)*, 1976. Gelatin silver print with oil paint, 14" x 11" (35.6 x 27.9 cm). Courtesy of the artist.

Comedy is an escape, not from truth but from despair; a narrow escape into faith.

Christopher Fry, b. 1907

English playwright

manipulated photography, changing the image in the darkroom or on the drawing board offers enormous potential for humor and subjective expression.

Straight photographs can be humorous when the photographer discovers unexpected situations or juxtapositions, or stages a humorous set-up for the camera. An example of staged photography is William Wegman's hilarious "dog pictures," in which he sets up a funny situation, using his Weimaraners as the subject. Judith Golden combines art and photography by painting directly on the finished print: "I think a photograph, whether it's set up or something you find in the world, has

Punnery and some fanciful embellishment of the human figure transform an ordinary subject into a surprising and surreal image. This is an example of staged photography—a creative set-up for the camera.

Judith Golden, *Carrot Top*, 1988. Cibachrome with dye, 20" x 16" (50.8 x 40.6 cm). Reprinted with permission of the artist.

Photomontage, as practiced by Uelsmann, is the technique of superimposing one image over another, so that the images are blended into a new composition. Uelsemann creates montages in the darkroom by either exposing printing paper to one or more negatives in succession, or by making a print from two or more sandwiched negatives.

Jerry Uelsmann, *Navigation Without Numbers*, 1971. Photomontage, 8" x 10" (20.3 x 25.4 cm). Courtesy of the artist.

a great deal of strength, because we as viewers accept it as reality. Even if it appears to be a very strange, magical phenomenon, we somehow accept it as *real* because it's in a photograph."[5]

Lazlo Moholy Nagy, Hannah Hoch, Raoul Hausmann, Alexander Rodchenko, and John Heartfield were Western artists of the early 1900s who similarly extended the boundaries of photography. Later, Robert Rauschenberg evolved a technique of *frottage* to transfer magazine and newspaper photographs to painting surfaces. He is among several artists including James Rosenquist, Andy Warhol, Audrey Flack, Patricia Nix, and Richard Hamilton who have combined photography and traditional art media in their work.

"It is photography," wrote Susan Sontag, in her book *On Photography*, "that has best shown how to juxtapose the sewing machine and the umbrella, whose fortuitous encounter was hailed by a great Surrealist poet as an epitome of the beautiful."[6] Surrealism, Cubism, Futurism, Constructivism, and Dadaism are art movements that inspired innovations in photography. Photo-collage, montage, camera-less photography (photograms), multiple exposure, the altered negative and print, the extreme close-up, the wide-angle and unusual-angle composition, nonobjective form, and mirror and lens distortion are some of the techniques and methods used by artists in this era. Multiple exposures with the camera and/or darkroom enlarger allows the artist further opportunities to transform images.

Other Photographic Innovations The use of sequential images, as in the comics, is a type of pictorial format often used by many contemporary photographers. Fragmentary and discontinuous arrangements are another way of grouping pictures and are often used to reflect the disjointed and hectic nature of the times.[7]

Much of today's contemporary art—particularly conceptual art, earth art, and performance art—is known principally by its photographic record. The Polaroid camera and photocopier have become standard art tools. The computer and its ever-evolving software further motivate the contemporary artist and the Sunday painter to digitize, morph, transform, transfigure, reconstruct—and "humorize"—photographic images.

Stop saying you're going to **take** pictures and say instead you're going to **make** them.
Ansel Adams, 20th-century American photographer

68

The Laughing Caricaturist

There are two basic types of caricaturists—the social caricaturist and the satirist. The social caricaturist creates benign, funny likenesses of subjects to entertain or appeal to the subject's ego. The satirist, on the other hand, produces caricatures that are designed to invoke thoughtful contemplation or inspire action on the part of the viewer. (See Chapter Four for more on caricature.)

Right:
David Levine, a preeminent figure in contemporary American caricature, has drawn caricatures for the *New York Review of Books* for thirty-one years.

David Levine, *Rembrandt van Rijn*, 1970. Reprinted with permission of the artist.

Below:
Luminaries of music are among Keenan's favorite subjects for caricature. Here the young Canadian artist captures the likeness and setting of Oscar Peterson, the world-renowned jazz pianist.

Pat Keenan, *Oscar,* 1994. Ceramic, 16" x 18" x 22" (40.6 x 45.7 x 55.9 cm). Webster Gallery, Calgary, Alberta.

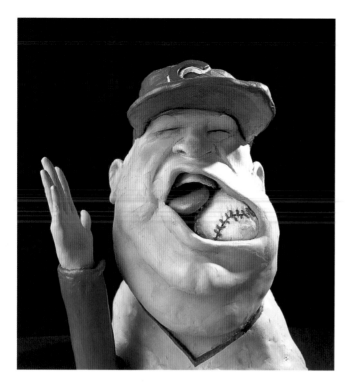

Don Zimmer is a legendary figure in baseball history and, as depicted in this caricature, a former manager of the Boston Red Sox.

Bob Selby, *Don Zimmer Talks Baseball*, 1989. Acrylic over clay. Courtesy of the artist and the *Providence Journal-Bulletin*.

The artist is a resident of Pense, Saskatchewan, a small community in the Canadian prairies. Fafard takes special pleasure in molding mini-likenesses of the local population in clay.

Joe Fafard, *Merchant of Pense*, 1973. Ceramic sculpture, 15" x 10" x 15" (38 x 25.4 x 38 cm). Susan Whitney Gallery, Regina, Saskatchewan.

The Cartoonist

The cartoonist, according to humor writer Harvey Weis, is a kind of wizard: "As a cartoonist, you can make people shrink, houses fly, ice cream cones explode, clouds turn into polka-dotted space craft—whatever you want. Ideas and imagination are the important things. Common sense and the laws of nature are of little concern."

Al Capp was one of the first comic-strip artists to defend the art of cartooning: "Genuine art today can be found in the comic strips. I judge comics by the same standard I apply to Daumier and Michelangelo." Indeed, comics are a viable form of artistic expression. Millions of people read comics daily. Children, adults, intellectuals, and nonintellectuals alike are comics addicts. Through the medium of humor, the cartoonist offers commentary, entertainment, instruction, release from tension, and historical perspective.

Cartoons can be broadly classified as: (1) the cartoon illustration, (2) the single-panel cartoon, (3) the narrative cartoon, and (4) the animated cartoon.

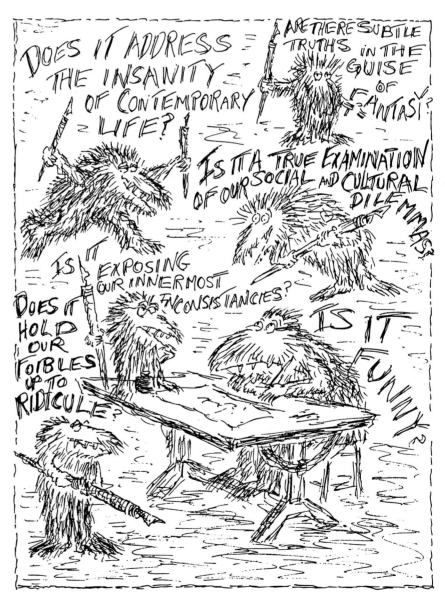

New Yorker artist Koren provides a humorous "how-to" treatise on creating visual humor, commencing with the fundamental question, "Does it address the insanity of contemporary life?"

Edward Koren, *Is It Funny?*, 1978. Pen and ink. Reprinted with permission of the artist.

Cartoon Illustration

The category of cartoon illustration includes *spot cartoons* (decorative drawings to fill space in magazines), *instructional illustration* (how-to representations), *story illustration* (as in children's books), and *advertising illustration* (cartoons designed to sell products in magazines, TV, or newspapers).

Single-panel Cartoons

Single-panel cartoons fall into two categories: humor cartoons, as featured in the *New Yorker* and other popular magazines, and editorial cartoons, which appear on the editorial page of the daily newspaper.

The single-panel cartoon is usually accompanied by text or speech balloons. The "silent" cartoon is without text and relies solely on visual imagery to convey its humor.

Since its inauguration in 1925, the *New Yorker* has been a showcase for single-panel cartoons and has introduced some of America's most popular cartoonists, including James Thurber, Peter Arno, Helen Hokinson, George Price, Eldon Dedini, Charles Addams, George Booth, Edward Koren, Mary Gauerk, Whitney Darrow, Jr., William Hamilton, Gluyas Williams, Mischa Richter, and Roz Chast.

Narrative Cartoons   Included within the narrative cartoon category is the comic strip and its varieties: the humor strip, the serial action-adventure strip, and the serial soap opera strip. Also in this genre is the comic book and its varieties—humor comics, adventure-crime comics, science fiction comics, "true" comics, and "love" comics. A strip is usually comprised of a series of cartoons showing humorous or adventurous happenings with a recurring cast of characters.

Comics are juxtaposed pictorial images set in sequence to tell a story—humorous or otherwise—and to evoke an emotional and aesthetic response. The basic difference between film animation and comics is that film animation is sequential in time but not spatially juxtaposed as comics are. According to Scott McCloud, author of *Understanding Comics*, "Each successive frame of a movie is projected on exactly the same space—the screen—while each frame of comics must occupy a different space."[8]

Unlike film art, the cartoonist does not show every single action but relies on the viewer's ability to complete mentally actions that occur between panels. Cartoonists call such subjective action between panels *closure*.

Pop culture, the love of the comics, and a love-hate struggle with food, prompted the artist to produce this manic food piece inspired by Dagwood's sandwich in Chic Young's comic strip, *Blondie* (created in 1930).

David Gilhooly, *Monumental Leaning Dagwood Sandwich*, 1984. Earthenware, glaze, 22" x 12" x 36" (55.9 x 30.5 x 91.4 cm). Courtesy of the artist.

Cartoon Animation

Cartoon Animation This genre of visual humor includes the *animated short*, the *animated instructional film*, the *animated feature film*, and the *animated commercial*.

Cartoonist Winsor McCay was the first American artist to produce animated cartoons. His classic films included *Little Nemo* (1910) and *Gertie the Dinosaur* (1914). Pat Sullivan and Otto Mesmer produced *Felix the Cat* in 1919, a popular series of animated cartoons.

It wasn't until Walt Disney created *Steamboat Willie* in 1928, which introduced Mickey Mouse, that a new innovation made its presence—the sound track. Disney's epic feature-length film, *Snow White and the Seven Dwarfs* (1937), is lauded even today as the best musical in Hollywood's history. Arguably, the most sophisticated animated cartoon feature is Disney's *Fantasia* (1940), using spectacular animation and classical music by Beethoven, Bach, and Stravinsky. Of recent vintage, Disney's popular features include *The Little Mermaid* (1989), *Beauty and the Beast* (1991), *Aladdin* (1992), *Pocahontas* (1995), *Toy Story* (1995), and *James and the Giant Peach* (1996).

Although the Disney corporation is still a dominant force in the industry, animated films are produced by individuals and organizations in many parts of the world other than Hollywood. George Dunning's

Timing—the number of drawings necessary to do the various movements—is something that must be mastered by the aspiring animator.

Harry Love
20th-century producer
Hanna-Barbera Studio

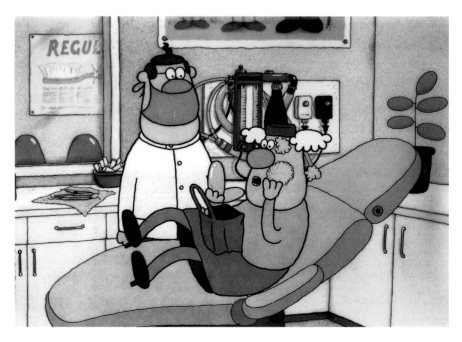

This animated film centers on the antics of a mild-mannered dentist who is depressed about turning forty. The film won an Oscar at the 1995 Academy Awards.

National Film Board of Canada, directors and writers: Alison Snowden, David Fine, *Bob's Birthday*, 1995. Film still.

Yellow Submarine, England (1968); Norman McLaren's experimental films sponsored by the National Film Board of Canada; and Joseph Kluge's and Hana Stepanova's, *The Gossips*, Czechoslovakia (1969), are a few of the excellent examples in this field.[9]

Cartoon animation is a labor-intensive process that involves the production of thousands of drawings that are photographed one frame at a time by the movie camera. Music and sound effects are added to fit the action and dialogue. The animation studio includes writers, storyboard artists, layout artists, animators, "cel" painters, background painters, musicians, photographers, directors, and producers who employ a wide variety of film techniques: stop-motion animation, live-action, and computer-generated effects. Recent advances in computer-generated imagery and digital effects have made a significant contribution to character animation, which is still largely hand-drawn.

In *The Lion King*—released by Walt Disney Studios in 1994—

Winsor McCay (1867–1934) was an influential and innovative genius in both the comic strip idiom and in the field of animation. His epic comic strip, *Little Nemo in Slumberland*, was first published in the *New York Herald* in 1905; his animated films predate Walt Disney's by twenty years. With unbridled use of fantasy and anthropomorphism, the artist narrated outlandish tales of humor and mirth.

Winsor McCay, *Little Nemo in Slumberland*, (detail) comic strip, 1908.

computer animation was used to create an incredibly realistic "wilde-beest stampede" that involves literally thousands of randomly moving animals—an action that would be almost impossible to accomplish without the aid of the computer.

In Richard William's animated film, *Who Framed Roger Rabbit?* (1988), an actor plays against a cartoon character. The coexistence of drawn and live characters in the same frames in *Roger Rabbit* is exceptionally well done. In *The Mask*, comedian Jim Carrey's face suddenly morphs into that of a cartoon wolf. The mind-boggling potential of computer-aided animation is only now beginning to emerge.

The Golden Age of Comics

The "golden age" of comic books spanned 1933 to 1948, a period that heralded such greats as *Superman, Batman, Archie, Pogo, Terry and the Pirates, Flash Gordon, Plastic Man, The Spirit, Wonder Woman, Mary Worth, Brenda Starr, Boots, Etta Kett, Juliet Jones,* and a host of animal comic books ranging from Mickey Mouse to Bugs Bunny—to name just a few. The legacy of these "golden oldies" lives on and many of them are reprinted for contemporary collectors. Today, young readers buy and enjoy the classics *Spiderman, Archie, Betty and Veronica,* along with new-comers such as *Sandman, Spawn, X-Man,* and *Power Rangers.*

The comic-book industry got into trouble during the 1940s and 1950s when its focus drifted to lurid, macabre, or sadistic stories, a circumstance that raised public indignation and eventually forced the

Hart never dreamed that the innocent joke in this cartoon could possibly offend anyone. Two editors for the *Arab News*, however, were sent to a Saudi Arabian prison for printing it, because officials believed the cartoon questioned the existence of God.

Johnny Hart, *God, If You're Up There, Give Me a Sign*, 1993. By permission of Johnny Hart and Creators Syndicate, Inc.

This montage of superheroes includes some of the characters McLaughlin has drawn for various comic books: Wonder Woman, Batman and Judo Master.

Frank McLaughlin, *Super Heroes*, 1977. Pen and ink. Reproduced with the permission of the artist.

The comic book artist must have the eye of a cinematographer, the soul of an actor, the precision of a director, the story sense of a writer—and the dedication of a monk.
Stan Lee, 20th-century American cartoonist

comic book industry to adopt a "Comics Code" in 1954. The code regulated the content of comic books and determined that publications would not contain scenes of violence, depravity, or sadism. Seventeen years later, however, the code was eased to allow the return of vampires, werewolves, psychological horror, and ultimately, the return of pictorial violence.

By way of reacting to censorship, a wave of underground comic books containing coarse humor came forth in the 1960s. Cartoonist Robert Crumb is perhaps the best-known artist of the underground

Robert Crumb, *Confessions of R. Crumb*, © 1968 R. Crumb. Reprinted by special permission of the artist.

comics of that era. Older readers and alternative-culture afficionados who enjoyed the underground comics (*Mad, Panic, Raw, Weirdo, Krazy Kat*, and the work of Robert Crumb) can find reprints from the old editions, but there is new comic surrealism available in *Heavy Metal, Eightball, Hate, Jimbo, Love and Rockets, Stickboy, Warts and All, Nexus, Bummer*, and *Doom Patrol*, to mention but a few of the many available titles.

Art Spiegelman's *Maus: A Survivor's Tale* is a masterful example of narration in the comic-book style. *Maus* was nominated for the National Book Critics Circle Award in biography in 1988 and heralded by critics as one of the greatest achievements in comic-book history of the previous twenty years. Based on his father's personal experience as a concentration camp survivor, Spiegelman narrates, in two volumes, the horror of the Holocaust. He uses animal "actors"—his father and other Jews were drawn as mice, the Nazis as cats. Comic books such as *Maus* demonstrate the tremendous potential of the comic book and its justifiable plea to be taken as a serious creative medium.

Will Eisner, a master cartoonist and parodist, has brought many innovations to the comic-book style and continues to entrance his readers with comic-book epics such as *City People Notebook*. *Moebius Comics* by

Jean Giraud and *Zippy* by Bill Griffith are also highly sought by collectors.

Japanese comics, particularly the Manga style, are enjoyed by an international audience. Japanese readers are known to buy over one billion comic magazines a year and may be the biggest consumers of the comics idiom.

Among European comics and cartoonists of note are *Tintin* by Herge, which is about the adventures of a boy reporter, and *Asterix,* by Rene Goscinny and Albert Uderzo, which is an opus on the life and times of Asterix and his sidekick Obelix as they travel through the Roman Empire.

The comic-book industry has also produced comic books derived from classic movies and literary classics. The influence of the comics is wide spread and can be observed in all genres of art and design.

Amiot's ceramic sculpture is inspired by the comics and the keen observation of the human comedy played out daily in city streets and public places. In this comic scenario the artist effectively uses *transposition*. The tableau depicts two errant hockey players in the penalty box—the confessional—doing penance for on-ice indiscretions.

Patrick Amiot, *Penalty Box*, 1994. Acrylic on clay, 11" x 16" x 8" (28 x 40.5 x 20 cm). Courtesy of the artist.

The Decline and Fall of the Comic Strip

Despite significant developments in printing technology, today's comic strips pale by comparison to those produced fifty years ago. No present-day comics are equal to the witty and beautifully drawn *Krazy Kat, Terry and the Pirates, Pogo* (see page 53), *Prince Valiant*, and *L'il Abner*, to mention but a few of the "golden oldies." The comic strip's attrition is due largely to the downsized, simplified, and overcrowded format typical of today's newspapers and tabloids. It is not uncommon to see twenty or more postage-stamp-size comics (roughly 1¾" x 5½") squeezed into the space of a single page—an uninviting clutter to say the least, not to mention the reduced legibility. The decline of the comics is exacerbated by newspaper editors who buy poorly drawn comics with trendy, "dumbed-down," puerile humor. Sadly, Bill Watterson's witty and well-drawn *Calvin and Hobbes* (see page 47), one of the best comics of the decade, was the latest to succumb to the menace of the shrinking page.

> The comic strip has endured by inventing complete, self-sustaining secondary worlds, where evil and suffering are either banished altogether or else represented in an unambiguously simplified and comprehensible form—so stylized and heightened that they transcend the moral muddle of caricature to attain the timeless clarity of myth or folktale.
>
> Adam Gopnik, 20th-century American art critic and staff writer for the New Yorker

Cartooning—Is It Art?

Bil Keane, the articulate creator of *Family Circus*, speaks for most cartoonists when he replied to this question in *Cartoonist Profiles*: "The comic strip is a brilliant form of art developed in America and now imitated in every country. More people see and appreciate this art form daily than ever see the expensive paintings tucked away in museums. I'm proud to be exhibited regularly in over 1300 newspapers, and to have my work hung on what I consider the world's most prestigious art gallery—the refrigerators in homes across America."

The presence of humor in any form is an indication of our emotional well-being. It is part of the process of our need for spiritual replenishment and freedom from boredom and automatic, robotic response. It is no wonder that the comic page is the first newspaper page to be read by millions daily. The antics of Calvin and Hobbes parody real life (Calvin: "I try to make everyone's day a little more surreal."); Dilbert's workplace makes anyone else's seem more tolerable; Linda Barry's *Ernie Pook's Comeek* reveals personal truths and angst we can all relate to; Cathy

Guisewite's *Cathy* and Lynn Johnston's *For Better or For Worse* are wonderful parodies of our social eccentricities, and *Garfield's* farcical encounters with sidekick Odie are pleasant diversions and flights of fantasy. The editorial cartoons by Herblock make us think and allow us to participate vicariously in politics.

The philosopher Ludwig Wittgenstein once said, "A serious work in philosophy could be written that consisted entirely of jokes." The same can be said for visual humor.

George Herriman, American cartoonist and creator of the famous comic strip *Krazy Kat,* is lauded by critics as a singular genius of comic strip fame. His zany, slapstick comics combine elements of poetry, whimsy, irony, philosophy, word play, and surrealism.

George Herriman, *Krazy Kat,* October 21, 1923. © King Features. Reprinted with special permission of King Features Syndicate.

Humor
That Bites

How I want thee, hum'rous Hogarth!
Thou, I hear, a pleasant rogue art.
Were but you and I acquainted,
ev'ry monster should be painted.
Jonathan Swift, 1667–1745
English (Irish-born) satirist

Chapter 4

Visual satire is a kind of oxymoron: It makes you laugh, but it isn't funny. In its mild form, *social parody*, it seeks to amuse by poking fun at society's idiosyncracies—its fads, fashions, behavior, and affectations. In its more trenchant form, *political satire*, it turns into a stinging assault. The artist's indignation is aroused by situations or ideas that are unjust, unworthy, or contemptible.

Political scientist Charles Press declares that all forms of graphic satire are alike insofar as they muse upon the ridiculous and the incongruous in life. The repeated theme in satirical art is the contrast between reality and the ideal, between aspiration and practice, between what *is* and what *could be*.[1]

Facing Page:
Albeit comic in appearance, the artist's work is a scathing indictment of human greed and dysfunction regarding ecological accountability. Fowler castigates the land developer who dishonors the land for economic gain. He is caricatured as an ogre who gobbles up bucolic greenery and spits out "concrete boxes."

Tim Fowler, *Real Estate Developer*, 1988. Painted wood, 45" x 10 1/2" x 20" (114.3 x 26.7 x 50.8 cm). On loan to the American Visionary Art Museum, Baltimore, from Brian Reagan. Photo by Allan Sprecher.

Moss is an editorial cartoonist for the *Washington Post*. Though his cartoons are captionless, the hybridized image of the *razor-pen* "speaks volumes."

Geoffrey Moss, *The Pen: A Lethal Weapon*. Reprinted by special permission of the artist.

Satire—Visual Protests and Playful Jests

From the universe of humor—wit, jocularity, farce, irony, parody, and caricature—the visual satirist fabricates and launches what might be called "the deadly humor missile." Its mission: to target and nullify human complacency, puffery, corruption, and demagoguery. Charles Philipon's famous cartoon of 1834, for example, depicts the French Citizen King Louis-Philippe metamorphosing into a pear. The word *poire* in French means "pear"—and "fathead."

Herblock (Herbert Block), political cartoonist for the *Washington Post*, explains that the mission of the political cartoonist is to poke fun

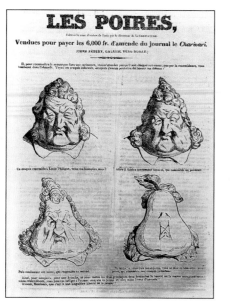

Philipon was publisher and occasional caricaturist of *Le Charivari*, a Parisian journal of the early 1800s, which was famous for its parody and satire of the French monarchy. In this cartoon, Philipon reduces the monarch Louis-Philippe to a *poire*—French slang for "fathead."

Charles Philipon, *Poire*, 1834. Metropolitan Museum of Art, New York.

"This work pretty much demonstrates what happens to smokers when they inhale," explains the artist. It is intended to serve as an advocate's message—delivered with a "sugar coating" of humor.

John Martin Gilbert, *Chain Smoker*, 1980. Mixed media, 12" x 12" x 4" (30.5 x 30.5 x 10.2 cm). Courtesy of the artist.

Appropriating themes from Greek and Italian art, Brown applies *transposition, contradiction,* and *parody* to produce an amiable, albeit cliché-ridden quip.

Chris Brown, *Venus de Credit*, 1994. Acrylic on canvas. Nicholas Treadwell Gallery, Bradford, Yorkshire, England.

and point out wrongs. "There are no sacred cows, and no matter how high the official, no sacred bull."[2]

Satire is sometimes labeled "negative art," but this designation is unfair since its *raison d'être* is often rooted in the belief in a more joyful life and a stable and lasting environment. Paradoxically, satire—whether obliquely caustic or explicitly vicious—is a way of getting at the truth.

The role of the satirist is to serve as a "public awakener" who has an avowed goal to communicate directly from one inward world to another in such a way as to render "a shock of experience." Visual satire ranges from a gentle wake-up call to an acrimonious whack. It can ravage like "a polished razor keen, which wounds with a touch that's hardly felt or seen," to quote poet Lady Mary Wortley Montagu, eighteenth-century British poet.[3] Aristotle put it well when he said wit, (particularly satire) is educated insolence.

Satire: the art which "afflicts the comfortable and comforts the afflicted."
H. L. Mencken, 1880–1956
American editor

The Designated Fool

Contemporary art critic Harold Rosenberg has written that artists do not protest because they think their protest is going to work, but because their conscience drives them to make a statement about conditions that are humanly intolerable. This role is not unlike that of the court jester or medieval clown who says what nobody else would dare to say, and does so because the role of clown is to be a representative of the truth.

Folly and seriousness can be thought of as two parts of an integrated whole. For example, the Feast of Fools was a widely celebrated occasion in Europe, wherein townsfolk and even pious priests donned bawdy masks, sang outrageous ditties, and committed themselves to revelry and satire.

The role of the designated fool in a variety of cultures has been to shake people up through high-spirited levity and to free them of apathy and depression. Some Native American cultures, for example, have a history of the "official fool" or "trickster" who acts contrary to custom by dressing funny, or walking and dancing backward. The Pueblo Clowns, for example, are revered by the tribe for their role in the balance of creation, reminding people of the path when they stray.

Gable uses *transposition* to portray *King Kong* atop a skyscraper, not to escape justice as in the classic movie, but to seek asylum from thugs in the metropolitan center.

Brian Gable, *Wreak Havoc and Distress?*, 1994. Reprinted with permission from *The Globe and Mail*.

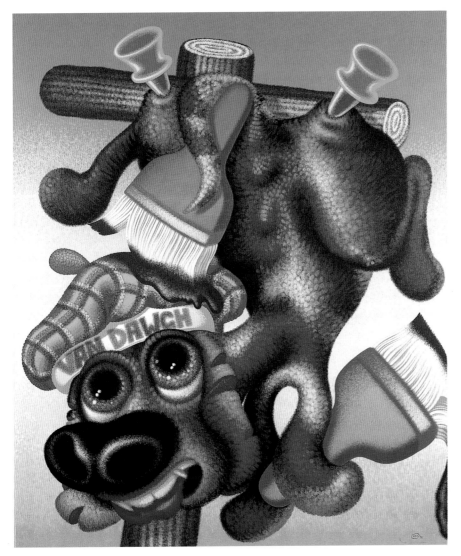

Nonsense or poignant metaphor? In his time Vincent van Gogh was considered an "outsider" and was "hung out to dry" by the art officialdom. Ironically, his canvases are among the most sought after (and costly) in today's market.

Peter Saul, *Vincent Van Dawgh*, 1988. Oil and acrylic on canvas, 90" x 72" (228.6 x 182.9 cm). Courtesy of the Frumkin/Adams Gallery, New York. Photo: Andre Grossmann.

Whether or not [art] will be effective as propaganda and make people change their opinion is a question more easily asked than answered. What the so-called editorial cartoon does is to provide some kind of momentary focus.

Ernst Gombrich, 20th-century art historian and iconologist

Unlike the dictionary definition, which describes a fool as one "who lives in a perpetual state of self deception," the wise fool is an idealist and visionary who mobilizes his or her wits to make people laugh and enjoy life. Such fools are cast in the Shakespearean tradition—wise enough to play the fool and possessed of a wit to do it well.

Visual humorists are visionary fools; they possess the imagination and wit to fabricate worlds that transcend reality, to generate playful disorder. Danish philosopher and theologian Sören Kierkegaard provided this analogy: "Satiric art is art-parable. It is the strategy of wounding from behind." Satire possesses a conscience-raising advocacy—a propaganda designed to convert thought and further causes of justice.

Early Satire

The Broadsheet

Printed sheets with "picture stories" were a popular medium of communication in "urban" Germany from the fifteenth to the seventeenth centuries, in Holland in the seventeenth century, and in England during the seventeenth and eighteenth centuries. The "broadsheet," as it came to be called in England, was a mass-produced handbill composed of engraved images and text, printed on cheap paper. Early broadsheets preached on Christian liturgical subjects, such as church doctrine, the Bible, the seven deadly sins, and the consequences of vice and folly. Later, they propagandized on social issues, crime and punishment, war, persecution, plots and revolutions, and political collusion.

Because these pictorial narratives were designed to educate and influence the thoughts of a wide spectrum of the middle- and lower-class populations in Europe, they were mostly pictorial, with a minimum of

This satirical illustration was used in *Mother Jones* (Aug. 1994) as an illustration for an article on the questionable procedures of commercial fishing.

Ray Troll, *Blues in the Key of Sea*, 1994. Reprinted with permission of the artist.

text. The aesthetic quality of the broadsheet was greatly enhanced in 1521 by Lucas Cranach, who satirized the papacy. Jacques Callot also produced trenchant images for the broadsheet in 1635, to serve as anti-war propaganda. Eventually, the broadsheet evolved into the *narrative album,* a suite of several sheets such as those popularized by William Hogarth.

Next, Satiric Caricature

Caricature is often defined as "mocking portraiture." (See the Caracci Family and Hogarth discussed in Chapter Two). Unlike the benign *portrait-chargé,* a form of caricature created mainly for the purpose of amusement in seventeenth-century Italy, satiric caricature is acerbic and

Tim Tolkein, *Big Shot*, 1987. Mixed media, metal, 15¾" x 15" x 19¾" (40 x 38 x 50 cm). Nicholas Treadwell Gallery, Bradford, Yorkshire, England.

English caricature thrived on satirizing the French Revolution and the Napoleonic wars. Gillray's visual humor was often aimed at skewering the "Corsican pest," Napoleon Bonaparte, portrayed by the satirist as "Little Boney."

James Gillray, *Corsican Pest*, 1803. Pen and ink, 9½" x 12¾" (24.1 x 32.4 cm). © British Museum.

The joke ought to be a learning process. The Zen masters knew this: the right riddle brings not only a laugh but enlightenment.

Richard von Buseck

20th-century, scientist

biting. By the end of the eighteenth century, caricature assumed the role of full-blown satire. It was English artist James Gillray who set the stage for this manifestation and is generally acknowledged as the founder of modern political satire. Gillray's caricature evolved from his fascination with English Romantic painting and the fanciful style of Henry Fuseli (a Swiss Romantic painter of the grotesque), which he merged into a unique style of satiric metaphor. The British caricaturists William Hogarth, Thomas Rowlandson, George Cruikshank, and their contemporaries (see Chapter Two) delighted in lampooning royalty, the military, the practices of medicine and law, morality, temperance, social abuses, pomposity, and the fads and fashion of the day.

Later, artists who used caricature as a style of painting and drawing ranged from post-Impressionists to German Expressionists, to Modernists. Toulouse-Lautrec, Max Beckmann, Edvard Munch, James Ensor, Otto Dix, Paul Klee, and Pablo Picasso are notables.

The Dada movement of the early 1920s inspired the admixture of caricature and fine art as revealed in the works by George Grosz and John Heartfield. (See the discussion of Dada in Chapter Five.)

Parody and Satire in Modern and Contemporary Art

Parody and satire differ in accordance with the amount of mockery or disdain in the artwork. Among notable contemporary visual parodists of this century are artists from the school of Social Realism, such as the American Ash Can painters who depicted daily life in the early 1900s. Ben Shahn, Grant Wood, Philip Evergood, and Jacob Lawrence were some of the artists who dedicated themselves to social parody.

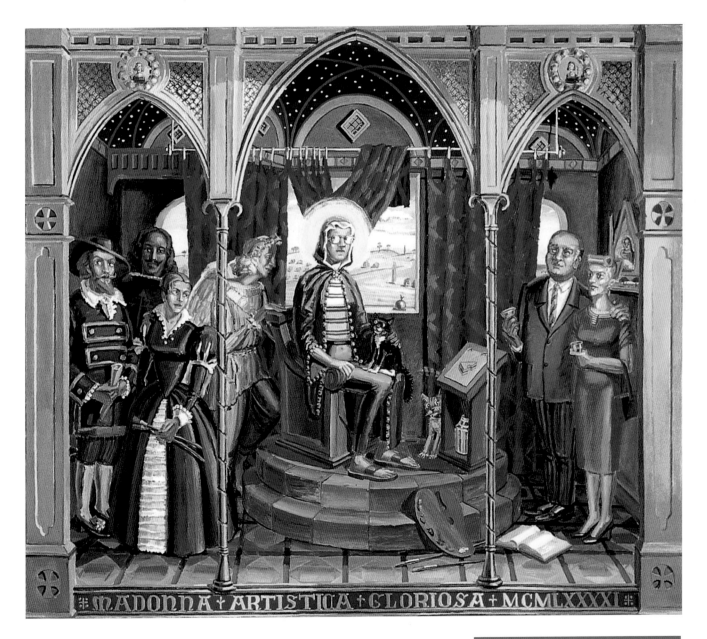

"This piece portrays an archetype figure—the typical long-winded public speaker. Any resemblance to persons living or dead is purely coincidental," says the artist. The artist adds, however, that he "was inspired to create this piece while listening to broadcasts from congressional hearings."

Sam Hernandez, *The Orator*, 1987. Wood, mixed media, 49" x 23" x 16" (124.5 x 58.4 x 40.6 cm). Photo by M. Lee Fatherree. Courtesy of the artist.

Among other social-realist painters of note are Reginald Marsh, who painted the tawdriness of city life; Paul Cadmus, who parodied urban life in the style of magic realism; Thomas Hart Benton, who satirized the "American scene"; William Gropper, who satirized capitalism; and the Mexican muralists José Clemente Orozco, David Siqueiros, and Diego Rivera, all of whom furthered revolutionary ideals through overt social satire.

Examples of satirical humor can be found in all of the major movements in American art—Pop Art, conceptual art, political art of the 1960s and 1970s, earth art, graffito, performance art, video art, installations, and so forth. Satire has invaded domains of both classical and contemporary art and has unabashedly mixed the sacred with the profane.

A Satirical Balance

The path for the satirical artist has never been smooth. The task of cutting through apathy is a tough and often exasperating venture. Graphic artist Milton Glaser states: "All issues that are truly profound—love, sex, death, and so on—become banal if they are expressed in a familiar way. If they are expressed in too novel a way you become terribly conscious of the author's cleverness as opposed to the essence of the idea. If you execute them with too much of a sense of horror, people turn off and they won't pay attention. It's essentially a question of getting the right balance between personal conviction and effective communication."

The use of the obvious metaphor, and cliché, typical in editorial cartooning and some political art, is required when the artist must ensure that the message will come through loud and clear. This "in-your-face" approach is favored by artists who believe that easily understood iconography and simplicity of design is the keystone to universal communication. This directness, however, is not without its problems. If clichés and puerile and simplistic ideas are used, there is the danger that the message will go unheeded.

An indirect approach couches ideas in double-entendre and oblique references through lesser-known metaphors and layered meanings. The use of layered meaning produces equivocality and turns the art into a

Shady dealing, corruption, and collusion among thugs and city hall officials was not uncommon in the early 1930s. Levine's self-designated role as "public awakener" prompted him to produce this satirical painting. The mocking title is taken from a passage in James Joyce's *Ulysses* wherein the protagonist is beaten by constables and loses his glasses and walking stick. A passerby who helps him to his feet says, "Your stick, sir." The man replies, "Stick? What need have I of a stick in this feast of pure reason?"

Jack Levine, *The Feast of Pure Reason*, 1937. Oil on canvas, 42" x 48" (106.7 x 121.9 cm). © 1996 The Museum of Modern Art, New York.

To young artists aspiring to expression in social or political commentary:

- Ideas come from information. Keep informed of current affairs.
- Further your education. Take additional courses; read up on historical events.
- Develop your drawing skills. Keep a sketchbook and draw continually from everyday subjects.
- Develop your sense of humor; study the work of editorial cartoonists and satirical artists, both past and present.

puzzle or riddle. The resolution of such seemingly puzzling art is not dependent on an awareness of universally known symbols, but rather on the personal and psychological associations and interpretations made by the viewer. Taken to extremes, this may also hinder communication.

Examples of the direct versus the indirect approach and the blend of cartooning and fine art are seen in Jack Levine's *The Feast of Pure Reason* (page 93) and James Ensor's *Skeletons Warming Themselves* (see page 37). Although both painters used a stylized form of pictorial expression, each used a contrary means for communicating his ideas. In *The Feast of Pure Reason*, Levine caricatures three figures: a crime boss, a wealthy politician, and a law-enforcement officer in what appears to be collusion. The message, which addresses problems of fraud and corruption in American life and politics, uses direct representation, that is, likenesses in the form of clichés, which are immediately recognized by the viewer.

On the other hand, the viewer must work harder to decipher the meanings in Ensor's *Skeletons*. The painting relies on symbolic representation. The tragic-comedic iconography presents skeletons as metaphors of a moribund society, the death of culture and the arts. The unlit lamp in Ensor's painting suggests that truth no longer shines.

Irony, contradiction, and satire are key humor-triggering mechanisms in this editorial cartoon.

Vance Rodewalt, *Playing Peacekeeper*, 1993. Brush and ink. Reprinted with permission of the artist.

Which Approach—On the Edge or Over It?

Kevin Kallaugher (a.k.a. KAL), editorial cartoonist for the *Baltimore Sun*, feels that political cartoonists must recognize the sensibilities of their readers. "You can't tick them off so much that they're not going to bother looking at you anymore. You want to tell them your point of view in a way that engages them, not just tell them they're jerks."

Though balance may be necessary in some situations, art that's on the edge or over it has a critical place in the world of ideas. Max Eastman in *Enjoyment of Laughter* discusses satire that goes over the edge: "Satire, if it is too bitter, runs out into hot scorn. There is a certain range of feelings which can be enjoyed playfully, just as certain wavelengths can be perceived as light, and if you pass beyond this laugh spectrum at either end the humor disappears. Once that fact is understood, the last pretext for identifying comic laughter as such with satire is removed. And it has to be removed before you can properly appreciate satire itself and the variety of its tones."[4] Taken over the edge and beyond, satire can become gallows humor—a morbid and depressive brand of jocularity with a black, sick, or truly tasteless nature.

Contemporary visual satirists whose imagery might be considered on the edge are Edward Kienholz and his wife Nancy Reddin, Robert Arneson, Steven Brodner, Geoffrey Moss, Ralph Steadman, Gerald Scarfe, Norman Catherine, and Dierdre Luzwick to mention but a few.

The job of political satirists is to revolt against complacency, indifference, and apathy to things that erode or threaten to destroy our personal freedoms and democratic way of life. "Make 'em laugh, make 'em think—and shake 'em up" is the battle cry of the political cartoonist.

Below:
Underlying the artist's sportive verbal-visual pun lurks a serious, subliminal message: "We are encroaching too much into wildlife habitats resulting in the devastating loss of biodiversity." National parks are so cluttered with human development that they are rapidly diminishing.

Anne Coe, *Counter Culture*, 1990. Acrylic on canvas, 50" x 70" (127 x 177.8 cm). Courtesy of the artist.

The artist portrays an evil warmonger by hybridizing human and monster characteristics. The exaggerated caricature borders on the grotesque, yet is a potent satirization.

Norman Catherine, *Dog of War*, 1988. Drypoint etching, 9⅞" x 12¼" (25 x 31 cm). Courtesy of the artist.

Pulitzer prize-winner Paul Conrad, cartoonist for the *Los Angeles Times*, gave a speech to fellow American political cartoonists in which he addressed the "dumbing down" of the contemporary political cartoon. He noted sadly that there is not enough edge in most of today's political cartoons and that artists are too soft on their subjects. "I see too much illustration of news stories today rather than editorial opinion. I'd like to see cartoonists get informed, get angry…and get to work!"[5]

Crossover Thoughts

For the satirist, iconoclasm is a job description. In North America, satire is still a proudly unregulated sport. As cartoonist Garry Trudeau points out, it is a sport with none of the normal rules of engagement; it picks a one-sided fight and is fully protected by the Constitution [and the Charter of Rights and Freedoms in Canada]. Granted that visual satire is a penetrating and effective form of criticism, a difficult question to answer is: At what point does it transcend comment and become art? Ralph E. Shikes, author of *The Indignant Eye*, proposes: "Probably when its drafts-

> Bombs and bombthrowers we've got, but where are those pie throwers?
>
> Melvin Maddocks
>
> 20th-century American writer

manship is superior and controlled, the composition inherently striking, the impact of the conception immediate, and the message of lasting interest."[6] As in all forms of creative art, the synthesis of craft, concept, and content are of paramount importance for the achievement of qualitative visual satire.

Hats off to the growing legion of parodists, satirists, lampoonists, and caricaturists who draw laughter from the spectacle of human events, from an estranged world that has become its own joke, where life often outstrips art in terms of farce and comedy. The advantage for the satirist who lives in a world where truth is usually stranger than fiction is that he or she need look no further than the local newspaper for subject matter. As the noted British author George Bernard Shaw perceptively noted, "My way of joking is to tell the truth. It's the funniest joke in the world!"

Below:
Couched in ironic humor and punnery is a deadly serious missive: "Our apathetic society allows profiteers to systematically destroy the natural environment."

Warrington Colescott, *Welcome to Watt Park*, 1984. Color etching, 24" x 35¾" (61 x 90.8 cm). Courtesy of the artist.

A Splendid Chaos

Lovers of nonsense enjoy brain-racking discord, the irresolvable conundrum, enigma, bewilderment, and the masochistic joy of having the rug pulled out from under them.

The dictionary defines nonsense as something that is "illogical, untrue, impractical," and "that which makes no sense." Dictionary definitions, however, don't deal with subjective or relative "truth." Thus, the perception and definition of nonsense varies from one person to another. To an artist, nonsense is not necessarily impractical but a form of creative expression or means of inspiring expression.

Facing Page:
Comic incongruity is produced by altering and/or displacing recognizable forms and objects from their normal context. Pratchenko adds to the enigma by pictorializing some eccentric characteristics of human perception. "The distortion prevalent in peripheral vision is actually the subject of this painting," he explains.

Paul Pratchenko, *Periphery*, 1989. Acrylic on canvas, 45" x 52" x 2 1/2" (114.3 x 132 x 6.35 cm). Courtesy of the artist.

Reminiscent of scenes from the Italian *commedia dell'arte*, Askin's inspired lunacy identifies him as a contemporary version of the court jester—the artist who endorses laughter as a religious experience and often offers merriment that veils thoughtful issues.

Walter Askin, *Stranded on a Lofty Premise by Changes in the Course of Vanguard Art While Critics Build Bridges to His Position*, 1978. Charcoal on Arches, 22" x 30" (55.8 x 76.2 cm). Courtesy of the artist.

DeForest's visual nonsense is at once startling and comically fascinating.

Roy DeForest, *Untitled (Marble Man)*, 1989–90. Acrylic on wood with mixed media, 69½" x 55" x 61" (176.5 x 139.7 x 155 cm). Rene and Veronica di Rosa Foundation, Napa, California.

True artists never see things as they really are...If they did, they would cease to be artists.

Oscar Wilde, 1854–1900

English (Irish-born) writer

Cassell's *Encyclopedia of Literature* says this: "The best way to describe nonsense is to say that it must be made with no ulterior purpose but to amuse by absurdity." Cassell's recognizes nonsense as something not lacking sense, but rather as a calculated effort to frustrate expectations *about* sense. Like other forms of humor, nonsense pivots on displaced logic, eccentric bisociation, distortion, ambiguity, punnery, and pseudo-profundity. What makes it different, however, from other forms of humor is that nonsense is based on *irresolvable* incongruity.

Making Sense of Nonsense

There is no such thing as nonsense, says Gary Zukav, author of *The Dancing Wu Li Masters*. "Nonsense" is that which does not fit into the prearranged patterns we have superimposed on reality. Zukav believes that the more clearly we experience something as "nonsense," the more clearly we are experiencing the boundaries of our self-imposed limitations. Nonsense is nonsense only when we have not yet found that point of view from which it makes sense.[1]

The Dutch humor researcher Hendrik van Leeuwen explains that the maker of nonsense enjoys playing with loose images, ordering them in an unexpected way, and tracing new and paradoxical modes of construction. Like an inventor, he or she makes discoveries while avoiding worn-out patterns and mental grooves.[2]

The artist's comic imagination evokes a three-dimensional, pseudoscientific mockup of the "inner workings of a hen." Note the built-in mechanism for decorating Easter eggs and the system for releasing the eggs from the "bomb bay."

John Martin Gilbert, *Inner Workings of a Hen*. (Gregory Peck), 1975. Mixed media, 8" x 8" x 6" (20.3 x 20.3 x 15.2 cm). Courtesy of the artist.

The British writer on Victorian fantasy, S. Prickett, explains that nonsense was probably created as an alternative language for coping with the conditions of a world at once more complicated and more repressive, "constituting an entire alternative aesthetic, making possible a radically different kind of art."[3]

A valid purpose of nonsense humor, therefore, is to offer artists new options for creativity and to challenge viewers to revise their definition of "Art." Nonsense can be accepted not as something that makes "no sense" but, as humor expert Wim Tiggs puts it, as a playful, pragmatic way of interpreting the universe.[4]

There was an Old Man of Coblenz,
The length of whose legs were immense;
He went with one prance, from Turkey to
*   France,*
That surprising Old Man of Coblenz.

Edward Lear, *There was an Old Man of Coblenz*, Limerick and illustration by Edward Lear, 1871. Courtesy of Faber and Faber, Ltd., London.

Ball works with found objects, natural materials, and artifacts. His images are drawn from influences of prehistoric, Romanesque, and medieval art.

Peter Eugene Ball, *Adam and Eve*, 1989. Wood/pewter, 24" (61 cm). Courtesy of the artist.

Poetic Dislocation

When people engage in humor, they collaborate in the production of "controlled absurdity." In nonsense humor, however, the accompanying perceptual tension generated by ambiguity is always sustained. The incongruity between order/disorder, illusion/reality, form/content, reason/emotion, free will/restraint, and so on, is never allowed resolution, as is the case with other forms of humor.

Nonsense humor is the art of "poetic dislocation" and is probably as old as language itself. As a genre, however, it came into popularity in the nineteenth century with the writing of Lewis Carroll (*Alice in Wonderland*) and the illustrated limericks of Edward Lear. A careful study of these Victorian works by humor researcher Elizabeth Sewell reveals that Carroll's and Lear's conception of nonsense is that of a carefully crafted and limited world, controlled and directed by reason and subject to its own laws. From this point of view nonsense is thought of as a self-referential game wherein the mind concocts an internal rationale and bizarre ways of making sense.[5]

As a form of comedic expression, nonsense seeks to balance a multiplicity of meaning with a simultaneous absence of meaning. This balance, according to Tiggs, is effected by tinkering with the rules of language, logic, and representation. The greater the distance or tension between what is presented, the expectations that are evoked, and the frustration of these expectations, the more nonsensical the effect will be.[6] Our first attempt to understand nonsense humor by rational means is naturally defeated, and we laugh when we realize finally that there is no logic to the joke, that it exists solely to defy reason. "Pragmatic people accept nonsense," explains novelist Anthony Burgess "hoping that experience will prove there is sense in it."[7]

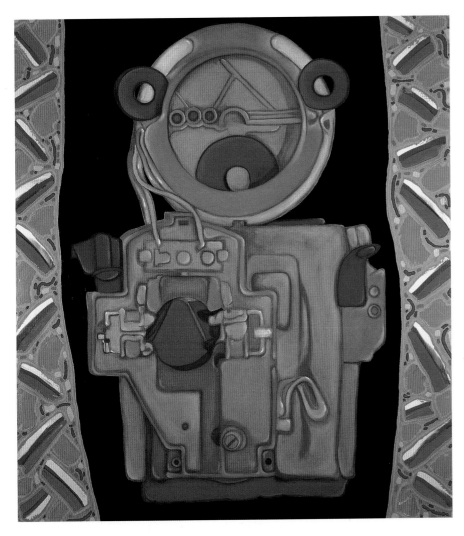

The term *grotesque* alludes to "that which is simultaneously humorous and frightening." Edwards' painting seems to satisfy the definition. The surreal image emerges from a preliminary composition—an assemblage of miscellaneous objects glued onto the surface of flat board. Edwards then used the assemblage as subject matter for the painting.

Stan Edwards, *Surveyor,* 1994. Oil and acrylic, 66" x 60" (167.6 x 152.4 cm). Courtesy of the artist.

And at night by the light of the
    Mulberry moon
They danced to the Flute of the
    Blue Baboon,
On the broad green leaves of the
    Crumpetty Tree,
And all were as happy as happy
    could be.
Edward Lear, 1812–1888
English painter and nonsense poet

Nonsense or Avant-garde?

Student: What's the difference between a monstrosity in art and a treasured masterpiece?

Professor of Art History: About fifty years.

The ridicule suffered by innovative artists is well documented in the journals of art history. In reviewing a painting by James McNeill Whistler, critic John Ruskin accused Whistler of "flinging a pot of paint in the public's face." At a trial in 1926, Constantin Brancusi's abstract bronze sculpture *Bird in Space*, shipped from Europe for an exhibition in New York, was declared by customs officials as "taxable metal"—not art. Time is the ultimate judge of creative accomplishments and has

The artist produces a verbal/visual pun by the literal interpretation of the word "dog-fight," normally alluding to aerial combat by flying aces such as the Red Baron and Eddie Rickenbacker.

John King, *Dogfight over Dogtown*, 1994. Oil on canvas, 40" x 40" (101.6 x 101.6 cm). Courtesy of the artist.

regularly vindicated artists who were hung out to dry by their peers in their own age.

History reminds us that people tend to laugh at or scoff at things that are new, because newness threatens comfortable conditioned responses. To begin to comprehend new ideas, people must work and think in unfamiliar ways. Richard Kostelanetz, in his book *Dictionary of the Avant-gardes*, explains: "One reason why avant-garde works should be initially hard to comprehend is not that they are intrinsically inscrutable or hermetic, but that they defy, or challenge as they defy, the perceptual procedures of artistically educated people. They forbid easy access or easy acceptance, as an audience perceives them as inexplicably different, if not forbiddingly revolutionary.[8]

The history of contemporary art—in all of its forms, from fine art to crafts, folk art and the comics—is a chronicle of destruction and rebirth, of conflicts, or as a psychologist might put it—of old gestalts giving way to new ones.

Toward Subjective Expression

The visual arts in the twentieth century are particularly distinctive in their shift from objective realism to psychological and metaphysical representation. With pronounced emphasis on self-discovery, many contemporary artists have explored the realm of the unconscious in an attempt to access subjective creativity.

The visual joke by David Gilhooly is born from idiosyncratic association, exaggeration, contradiction, parody, and pseudorepresentation of historical artifacts.

David Gilhooly, *Formal Totem Pole*, 1993. Ceramic, 22" x 16" x 40" (55.8 x 40.6 x 101.6 cm). Courtesy of the artist.

This object attempts to fool us into thinking that it is a team of horses and a carriage. The ingenious nonsense recalls the words of René Magritte: "We seem to be seeing images that bypass the old order of art altogether to come into direct contact with the primal, pre-rational, symbolic vision of the unconscious."

Pascale Galipeau, *Monture Mariale pour L'Ascension de Soi-meme*, 1988. Found materials, mixed media, 11¾" x 7⅞" x 27½" (30 x 20 x 70 cm). Courtesy of the artist.

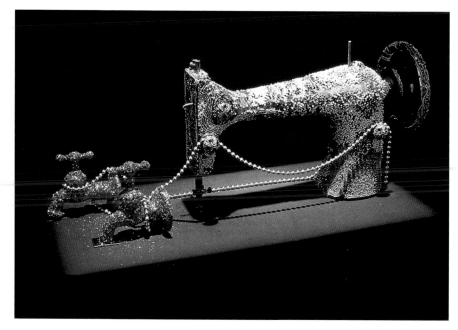

The irrational art of Surrealism made its debut in 1924, but before its appearance, subjectivism was a central concern to many artists who sought to pictorialize emotional and psychological sensations. Among them are:

- **John Henry Fuseli** (1741–1825) of Zurich, a painter of the fantastic, grotesque, dreamy and nightmarish.
- **Odilon Redon** (1840–1916), French artist and symbolist who made graphic representations of dreamlike scenes populated by weird amoeboid creatures.
- **Giorgio de Chirico** (1888–1978), Greek-born artist who painted enigmatic pictures and sought to access the realm of the metaphysical by placing ordinary objects in new and mysterious relationships. De Chirico once said, "One must not forget that a picture should always be the reflection of a profound sensation, and that profound signifies strange, and strange signifies the little known or entirely unknown."[9]
- **Marc Chagall** (1889–1985), a painter of joyous, romantic love and personal memories, often portraying simultaneous recollections tinged with passion, angst, and humor.
- **Paul Klee** (1879–1940), Swiss painter and instructor at the German Bauhaus Academy, and a principal exponent of psychic expression.

Klee was one of the most inventive and prolific artists of his time. Subjective expression, in Klee's words, marked the beginning of the exploration of the "between world," the realm between dream and reality. His *Pedagogical Sketchbook* (1953) is an inspirational text for students of art.[10] (See *Twittering Machine*, page 41.)

- **Henri Matisse** (1869–1954), initially a Fauvist painter, who provided followers with a new motive for creativity when he said, "Art is not in copying the object but rather in realizing one's sensations through it."

- **Franz Marc** (1880–1916), one of the founders of the German Blaue Reiter. Marc pursued a subjective and highly expressionistic approach by doing a series of animal paintings in 1911 titled *The Great Blue Horses*, using "unrealistic" bright primary colors, rather than the "natural" colors associated with horses.

- **Pablo Picasso** (1881–1973), influential in the evolution of most manifestations of modern art in the 1900s. His outrageous use of non-Western influences, particularly African masks, in figurative art was a truly inspired milestone in art history. (See pages 14 and 18.)

All of the foregoing artists (and others whom space precludes mentioning) played a significant role in the unfolding of subjective representation in fine art and in setting the stage for two "irrational" art movements that followed.

Freedom from Art, Freedom for Art: Dada and Surrealism

The years 1915–1924 saw the evolution of two remarkable and seemingly irrational manifestations in art: Dada and Surrealism. Although both movements relied on the irrational, Dada was a negative, anti-art movement, whereas Surrealism was based on the search for expanded avenues of expression.

Below:
Cicansky's visual joke spins out of idiosyncratic parody—a farcical coupling of image and title.

Victor Cicansky, *Ménage à Trois*, 1994. Clay and glaze, 7⅞" x 7⅞" x 7⅞" (20 x 20 x 20 cm). Susan Whitney Gallery, Regina, Saskatchewan.

Dada—Nihilistic Expression

Dada—the infamous, anarchistic movement of the early 1900s—began in Zurich by artists disillusioned with the horrors of mass production and war on a massive scale. The Dadaists blamed society, particularly the scientific and technological community, for eroding European life and unleashing the devastating terror of World War I. Their revolt spread to New York and Barcelona, then to Berlin, Cologne, and Paris. It gave rise to a form of irrational humor based on free association and is epitomized in the remarks by the artist Marcel Duchamp, who said that all one needs to do to instantly "aestheticize" an object—even if the object happens to be some discarded junk—is simply to place it in a museum and declare it "Art."

In 1913, art critic and poet Guillaume Apollinaire provided Dadaists with some surprising "tools" for visual expression when he announced: "You may paint with whatever material you please; with pipes, postage stamps, postcards or playing cards, pieces of cloth, painted papers or newspapers." Absurd poetry readings, "noise-music," and miscellaneous acts of tomfoolery were regularly performed by Dadaists to shock and outrage the public. The automatic and chance methods used by these artists are reminiscent of an exchange between Alessandro Botticelli (1445–1510) and Leonardo da Vinci. Botticelli facetiously remarked that by throwing a sponge soaked with different colors at a wall one can make a spot in which a beautiful landscape can be seen. Da Vinci, offended by the remark, replied that one can indeed learn much from chance configurations and that he in fact encourages his students to study the stains on walls and buildings for latent images and designs.

Three Dada-inspired techniques are *frottage*, *décalcomanie*, and *fumage*. *Frottage*, developed by Max Ernst, involves a method of producing designs from rubbings of textured materials. *Decalcomania*, also advanced by Ernst, involves wet blobs of paint squeezed between two sur-

Duchamp invented the "ready-made" and was a provocateur who declared that any object selected from the limbo of unregarded objects becomes a work of art on the artist's say-so.

Marcel Duchamp, *Bicycle Wheel*, 1951 (Third version after lost original created in 1913). Assemblage: metal wheel, mounted on painted wood stool, 50 1/2" x 25 1/2" x 16 5/8" (128.3 x 64.8 x 42.2 cm). Museum of Modern Art, New York.

Hogarth presents amusing perceptual ambiguities, a composition stuffed with visual anachronisms and bizarre representations.

William Hogarth, *Fisherman*, 1754. Engraving, 8¼" x 6⅞" (21 x 17.5 cm). British Museum.

faces, which are then manipulated by pressure and separated to produce bizarre random patterns. *Fumage,* developed by the Austrian-Mexican painter Wolfgang Paalen (1907–1959), is the process of moving a freshly primed canvas perpendicularly over a candle flame to produce smoke patterns in its wet surface. The patterns are used to inspire further designs by the artist, who then spontaneously paints onto the wet surface with oil paints.

Although Dada was an international expression that denounced art movements and bourgeois values, its impact brought about an extraordinary number of new modes of expression for art. These include stream-of-consciousness writing or automatic writing, concrete poetry, chance art, collage, photomontage, assemblage, abstract relief sculpture, abstract film, found-object art, happenings, installation art, and surreal imagery. Of particular significance, Dada brought forth the art of the *bricoleur*—the artist who transforms discarded objects and paraphernalia into something of added meaning. The absurdity of Dada inspired the freedom to find new visual relations through chance, "accident," and other serendipitous procedures, which, in turn, inspired surrealistic art.

Surrealism—Irrational Ingenuity

Surrealism became a dominant international force in arts and literature from the mid-1920s to 1940s. Some of its practitioners were Jean Arp and Max Ernst (Germany); René Magritte (Belgium); Pablo Picasso, Joan Miró, and Salvador Dali (Spain); Meret Oppenheim (Switzerland); André Masson, Man Ray, and Yves Tanguy (France); Frida Kahlo and Remedios Varo (Mexico); and Matta (Chile).

Oppenheim's formula for "making the familiar strange" is based on her simple premise: Select a commonplace object and "*do* something to it." The manipulation of found objects was commonly used by Dada and Surrealist artists.

Meret Oppenheim, *Object (Luncheon in Fur)*, 1936. Fur-covered cup, saucer, and spoon, height: 2 7/8" (7.3 cm). Museum of Modern Art, New York.

Although as a movement Surrealism no longer exists, its impact and spirit are alive in the work of many contemporary artists. Surreality, according to its founder, André Breton, is a resolution of dream and reality and therefore "an expansion of reality." Surrealists sought an expansion of reality through psychic awareness and access to the unconscious and dream state. Chance procedures and fantastic juxtapositions were the means to surreal images. Through the presentation of the seemingly irrational, Surrealists strove to surprise, disturb, and educate viewers into new modes of awareness.

Surrealism exploits the visual oxymoron, an *oxymoron* being something that is self-contradictory. In literature, for example, the terms *loud silence, foolishly wise, clear as mud, like a lead balloon* are antithetical expressions. The visual oxymoron is art's counterpart. Technically, *any* kind of design that presents perceptual contradiction is an oxymoron. The category includes optical illusions, puns, double-entendres, non sequiturs, and surreal art.

Meret Oppenheim's fur-covered cup, René Magritte's *The Treachery of Images (This is not a pipe)* (see page 8), Salvador Dali's *The Persistence of*

Surrealist painter René Magritte engages a style of convincing realism that is coupled with an incongruous juxtaposition of mundane objects. The unification of objective realism and fantasy in the image tend to make the illusion appear credible. Yet, when the logic-seeking brain detects the futility of any rational conciliation, it might react to it in the same way it does when confronted with nonsense jokes—with laughter.

René Magritte, *Time Transfixed (La Durée Poignardée)*, 1939. Oil on canvas, 57⅜" x 38⅜" (146.4 x 97.5 cm). The Art Institute of Chicago.

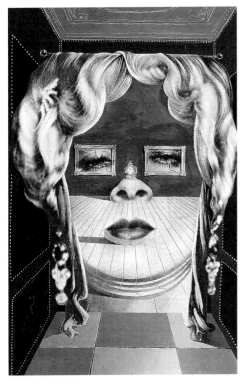

Multiple images, optical illusion, surreal art, and humor are skillfully interwoven to produce an amusing, albeit perceptually equivocal portrait of the well-known actress of the silver screen.

Salvador Dali, *The Face of Mae West*, 1934–1935. Oil on canvas, gouache on newspaper, 10⅞ x 6⅞" (27.6 x 17.5 cm). Courtesy of the Art Institute of Chicago.

Memory, Man Ray's *Gift* (flatiron with nails), and M.C. Escher's *Autographic Hands* are classic examples of the visual oxymoron in art. Magritte's surreal painting, *Time Transfixed*, is a startling image, in that unlike dream images that are fleeting and ephemeral are fixed permanently in objective reality. Contemporary artist Mike Thaler (see drawings below) is unique in his invention of funny visual oxymorons.

Surrealist art is often funny because, like all forms of comedy, it is allied to the discontinuous. Man Ray's humor evolves from the procedure of interrupting rational order and shifting viewers' perspective to suggest that certain incongruously juxtaposed objects belong together.

Man Ray, *Gift* (replica of 1921 original). Painted flatiron with a row of thirteen tacks, 6¼" x 3⅝" x 4½" (15.3 x 9 x 11.4 cm). The Museum of Modern Art, New York, James Thrall Soby Fund.

Naive and Pseudo-Naive Nonsense

The term *outsider art* refers to the creativity of self-taught individuals who've had no art school training or have had no exposure to mainstream art and culture. This category of artists includes naive, folk, or tribal artists, art by those who have been labeled "schizophrenic" and "psychotic," and artist/visionaries who create bizarre environments.

Jean Dubuffet coined the term *Art Brut* to describe a style of rough, "raw art"—art that is simple in form and is spontaneous. Pseudo-naive artists, such as Paul Klee, Jean Dubuffet, Karel Appel, Enrico Baj, and Alden Mason were influenced by genuine outsider artists, such as the self-taught Henri Rousseau, and by the schools of Expressionism, Surrealism, and Primitivism. Among the contemporary pseudo-naive artists are the 1960s graduates of the School of the Art Institute of Chicago (*Hairy Who*): Karl Wirsum, Jim Nutt, and Gladys Nilsson, among others.

A Pianoceros

An Oboe Constrictor

Turtle Drums

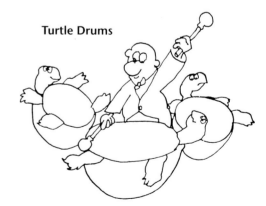

Puns, malapropisms, and spoonerisms provide raw material for visual wit and punnery.

Mike Thaler, *Visual Puns*, 1995. Courtesy of the artist.

Visionary environments include Simon Rodia's *Watts Towers* in Los Angeles, Antoni Gaudi's *Church of the Sagrada Familia* and his *Parque Guell* in Barcelona, and Ferdinand Cheval's *Palais Idéal* in Hauterives, France. Also in this category of bizarre architectural habitats is the fantastic architectural-sized sculpture of Niki de Saint Phalle (the *Nanas*) and Paolo Soleri's *Arcosanti,* a utopian village set in the Arizona desert. All of these fantastic structures have one thing in common: a wholesale abandon of traditional standards.

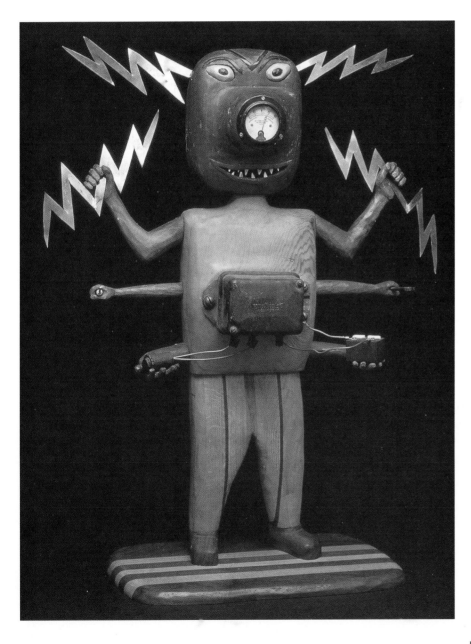

Characterizing his work as "carvings of occupation gods," Tim Fowler, a self-taught artist, comments, "Volt God is inspired by the never-ending trial of keeping old vehicles in running order." The viewer might interpret the piece as a satirical comment on power-wielding social, political, or military figures, or perhaps as a "creativity muse," equipped with lightning bolts of ideas to fling at artists in need of creative inspiration.

Tim Fowler, *Volt God*, 1995. Mixed media, 12" high (30.5 cm). American Visionary Museum, Baltimore. Photo by Allan Sprecher.

Krazy Kat, created in 1910, ranks among the funniest and most inspired creations in the comic-strip genre. The comic's cast of characters include Krazy Kat, Ignatz Mouse, and Officer Pupp, whose actions include total nonsense and brick throwing. The pun-laden strip amused a faithful audience for over thirty years.

George Herriman, *Krazy Kat: Twenty Billow* (frame). Reprinted with special permission of King Features Syndicate.

Ignatz: The World as it is, my dear "K," is not like it was when it used to be.

Krazy: An' w'en it get to be wot it is—will it?

George Herriman, 1880–1944
Pioneer comic-strip artist and creator of Krazy Kat

Nonsense and Cartoon Fantasy

Cartoon fantasy is not limited solely to the so-called "low art" of the funny papers. Picasso, Klee, Miró, and Feininger are but a few of the modernists who used caricature and cartoonlike illustration in painting and sculpture. In today's art world, Gladys Nilsson, Barbara Rossi, Christina Ramberg, Jim Nutt, Karl Wirsum, Peter Saul, Kenny Sharf, Jeff Koons, Keith Haring, Robert Arneson, David Gilhooly, Mick Sheldon, William Snyder, Clayton Bailey, and Marcus Pierson are among the many artists who have combined surrealism and a cartoon style in fine art.

Comics Surrealism

Little Nemo in Slumberland, created by Winsor McCay in 1905 (see page 75), was one of the first American comic strips. It was based on surreal plots in which a boy named Nemo is whisked into fantastic voyages every night while dreaming. George Herriman's *Krazy Kat*, created in 1910, is a hilariously funny surreal comic strip that has captured the attention of fine artists such as Joan Miró, Willem DeKooning, Picasso, and Öyvind Fahlström. Rodolphe Dirk's *Katzenjammer Kids*, created in 1896 and one of the longest running comics, provides humor in the

form of horseplay and nonsense. Rube Goldberg's *Foolish Inventions* (1914) presents farcical expositions of nonsensical futuristic inventions. Surreality rises to an art in comic books such as *Buck Rogers, Spiderman, Plasticman, Tales of the Unexpected, Weird Fantasy*, and *Mad*, to mention only a few from the hundreds of contemporary titles.

Nightmarish fantasy with a psychopathic overtone might best describe the cartoons of Robert Crumb, a pioneer of the underground comics of the 1960s (see page 78). Crumb's explicit treatment of social dysfunction, drugs, sex, the decay of spiritual values, and rebellious youth largely defined the underground comics and the counterculture of his day. His often reprinted cartoons are seen in comic books such as *Zap, Uneeda, Weirdo,* and *XYZ Comics.* Interestingly, Crumb's disillusionment, grotesquery, and tragic-comedic cartoon style has been paraphrased by fine artists such as Philip Guston and Peter Saul.

Rube Goldberg was noted for his complex and utterly utopian inventions. Here's how the outboard motor that requires no fuel works: As you reach for the anchor, button (A) snaps loose and hits spigot (B), causing beer to run into pail (C). Weight pulls cord (D), firing shotgun (E). Report frightens sea gull (F), which flies away and causes ice (G) to lower in front of false teeth (H). As teeth chatter from cold they bite cord (I) in half, allowing pointed tool (J) to drop and rip bag of corn (K). Corn falls into net (L). Weight causes it to snap latch, opening floor of cage (M) and dropping duck into shafts (N). As duck (O) tries to reach corn it swims and causes canoe to move ahead.

Rube Goldberg, Outboard Motor That Requires No Fuel (Nutty Inventions series), 1914. © Rube Goldberg Inc. Courtesy of United Feature Syndicate.

The brightly colored construction is playlike in form, brightly colored, and casts a historical reference to the styles of Constructivism, Art Deco, and Surrealism. Miniature tables, chairs, stairs, and ladders are scattered throughout this three-dimensional construction along with diminutive, anthropomorphic shapes that "people the architectural space." Kostiniuk explains that although his sculpture has a cheery and lighthearted quality, it actually "speaks symbolically to human conditions and circumstances that tend to minimize and depreciate people's lives."

Ron Kostiniuk, *Celia's Casa*, 1987. Enamel and aluminum and wood, 24" x 48" x 33" (61 x 121.9 x 83.8 cm). Courtesy of the artist.

The Beat Goes On

The tradition of fantasy, grotesquery, nonsense, and irrationality will continue to have a prominent place in creative expression. Artists who combine humor and nonsense in their work are important because they have brought a breath of fresh air to the art world. Our need for absurdity and laughter is well expressed in the mandate of the Just for Laughs Museum in Montreal, Quebec: "We have come to realize that beyond common sense lies a universe of utter chaos, unrelieved nonsense and riotous freedom of expression. Under their influence, our universe is refreshed, and we begin to reinvent our relation to the world."

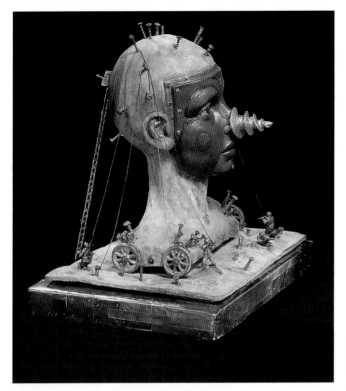

Cohen's style might be described as comic surrealism, a style that blends objective reality with mythology and flights of fancy. "To be able to see my dreams and fantasies in tangible form is for me what [creativity] is all about."

Claudia Cohen, *Just Plane Screwy*, 1992. Clay and mixed media, 16" x 18" x 12" (40.6 x 45.7 x 30.5 cm). Courtesy of the artist.

The title of this work, *Incognito Ergo Sum* is a play on words on Descartes' premise, *Cognito Ergo Sum (I think, therefore I am)*.

Ginny Ruffner, *Envisioning Series: Incognito Ergo Sum*, 1995. Glass and mixed media, 12" x 7.5" x 7" (30.5 x 19 x 17.8 cm). Courtesy of the artist.

Humorobics

"The time has come," the walrus said,

"To talk of many things:

of shoes—and ships—and sealing wax—

Of cabbages and kings…"

Lewis Carroll, *Alice in Wonderland*

First published in 1865

Chapter 6

The creation of visual humor is analogous to making an omelet. You can't make an omelet without cracking eggs, just as you can't create humor without breaking stereotypes or expectations. Now it's time to turn theory into practice and crack a few eggs. This chapter's activities trigger the comic imagination by encouraging free association and unorthodox thinking. Transform your studio or classroom into a laughter workshop. Be inventive; tailor the suggested activities in this chapter to suit your specific needs or the needs and abilities of your students, and create your own humorobics.[1]

Facing Page:
Haberman's forte is in three-dimensional cartoon tableaus that parody social events. Haberman forms bakeable clay and further refines it by sanding and then painting it with water-based acrylics.

Jim Haberman, *Surf City*, 1988. Mixed media. Installation and photograph by the artist, 1988 © Jim Haberman.

The artist explains that this work was inspired by an ambiguously funny remark by George Bush during the 1988 presidential election campaign: "We will never use food as a weapon."

Craig Nutt, *We Will Never Use Food as a Weapon (Carrot Bomb)*, 1989. Oil paint on carved tupelo and poplar, 24" x 15" x 20" (61 x 38 x 50.8 cm). Photo: Rickey Yanura.

Exercising the Funny Bone

The humor-triggering mechanisms introduced in Chapter One are repeated here for easy reference. Note that humor-triggering mechanisms don't always work alone but in concert with other mechanisms.

Association Combination, alliance, connection, juxtaposition, comparison, analogy, metaphor, superimposition, coalescence

Transposition Shift, transference, switch, adaptation, dislocation, relocation, substitution, translation

Transformation Change, evolution, progression, transmutation, metamorphosis, hybridization, anthropomorphism

Contradiction Contrariety, reversal, oppositeness, irony, incongruity, ambiguity, paradox, surprise

Exaggeration Overstatement, (or understatement), caricature, prevarication, stretching the truth, fibbing, joking, tomfoolery, absurdity, irrationality

Parody Mimicry, burlesque, spoof, comic interpretation

Randy Glasbergen, *Barbells,* 1994. Pen and ink. Reprinted with permission of the artist.

Pierson's coyote is a funny anthropomorphic emissary of his alter ego. The coyote is a man-beast hybrid that originated in 1986 when the artist heard Joni Mitchell's song of the same name. The tune inspired him to create a kind of "reckless, dangerous type of character" that he casts in amusing tableaus.

Marcus Pierson, *Wild Ones*. Cast epoxy. © 1995 Out West Inc. All rights reserved.

Pun Word play, word/image play, comic ambiguity, double meaning, adage, joke, spoonerism, malapropism

Disguise Concealment, deception, camouflage, illusion, riddle

Satire Lampoonery, raillery, ridicule

Narration Storytelling, presentation of action or events, sequenced graphic representation, cartooning

Appropriation Borrowing, taking, annexing, conscripting, quoting, referring

Association

It's impossible to make a noise by clapping the air with just one hand. Likewise, the artist cannot create visual humor by attempting to "clap" with only a single element. Only by thoughtfully arranging, associating, and connecting disparate elements can new ideas and structures be produced. "Forced" association produces *synergy,* in which the total effect is greater than the sum of its parts.

Photographs, mixed media, and hand-drawn details in pen and ink are combined in creating this image. The artist cleverly uses a toilet bowl brush for the character's beard.

Richard Newman, *Bacchus,* 1974. Photo montage, 18" x 14" (45.7 x 35.5 cm). Courtesy of the artist.

Fantasy Face

A good way to begin the exploration of visual humor is by making humorous fantasy faces. Select one or more of the following ways for your designs.

Collage: Arrange and paste disparate cutout shapes and images from magazines and newspapers onto a suitable sheet of colored construction paper.

Bas-relief: Assemble and glue three-dimensional materials onto a background of heavy cardboard or presswood panel.

Sculpture: Combine odd pieces of junk or "derelict" objects to make a portrait. Or arrange and glue images and cutout shapes from magazines onto a three-dimensional object.

Obviously realistic contingencies are necessary not just for creativity but for every form of life.
Silvano Arieti, 20th-century
American psychologist and writer on creativity

Michael Stevens, *House of Frankenstein,* 1989. Pine, enamel, plastic, mixed media. 75" x 25" x 16" (190.5 x 63.5 x 40.6 cm). Courtesy of the Braunstein-Quay Gallery, San Francisco.

Fantasy Critter

With a drawing material of your choice, manipulate the basic elements of art—line, shape, form, and color—to produce an amusing, preposterous creature. Don't worry about making it "real." Keep in mind the words of creativity expert Silvano Arieti: "The artist possesses the ability to transcend reality to put together elements that are not together in the external world."[2]

"It's fun to work with old stuff to make something out of it," says this self-taught artist. Strickland recycles old farm equipment, auto parts, air-conditioning duct work, and miscellaneous detritus to weld fanciful creatures, birds, animals, and people.

David Strickland, *Big Bird*, 1990. Metal, 58" x 52" x 55" (147.3 x 132 x 139.7 cm). New Orleans Museum of Art. Collection of Mrs. Sally Griffiths.

Association Exercise 3
Funny Human Figure
Select an archetype, such as the *artist, musician, doctor, scientist, lover, athlete, actor,* and so forth. Explore farcical representation by using caricature, exaggeration, and absurdity to make an amusing human figure. Combine outlandish shapes and forms and unusual elements to make a figure from papier-mâché, clay, or assembled found objects.

Association Exercise 4
Fantasy Scenario
Take the concept of association to the limits. With a pun or humorous idea in mind, arrange some funny figures in a funny situation. Work in either a two- or three-dimensional mode, seeking to produce surprise and incongruity. Other humor-triggering mechanisms to consider: exaggeration, parody, or satire.

Below:
Armed with puns, malapropisms, spoonerisms, and other forms of visual-verbal errata, the artist prompts humor and art to coexist.

Tom Foolery, *Jurassic Classic, On the Rodin Again,* 1981. Assemblage, 10" x 12" x 12" (25.4 x 30.5 x 30.5 cm). Courtesy of the artist.

Transposition

Wildly funny and absurd conceptions and metaphors are readily produced by transferring the context of an image or idea from one frame of reference to another. Mix and match subjects from different time frames and realms of knowledge from history, literature, science, biology, botany, philosophy, and art.

Ideas and bizarre images readily issue from *displacement* (imagine Socrates on roller blades), *interpolation* (Mickey Mouse in the boat with George Washington crossing the Delaware), *hybridization* (ear of corn as a taxicab) and *anthropomorphism* (vacuum cleaner, toaster, and TV engaged in philosophical conversation). Transposition allows the artist to switch, shift, substitute, and dislocate—and thereby make the impossible possible.

Berti uses mock archaeology to "relocate" any mundane object into fantasy time and space. Berti's image, a baseball and glove skillfully carved in stone, attempts to fool us into thinking that it's a genuine archaeological discovery.

Chris Berti, *Safe at Home.* Limestone, 12" x 19" x 17" (30.5 x 48.3 x 43.2 cm). Courtesy of Robert Kidd Gallery.

Dislocation

Transpose, or relocate, an everyday object from its normal environment to a bizarre or irrational place. Use a selected two- or three-dimensional medium to realize your idea. Other mechanisms spark inspiration: switching, substitution, transformation, and metamorphosis.

The humor-triggering mechanisms *transposition, dislocation,* and *contradiction* are used to produce an intelligible narrative. The illustration was used in a Diners Club magazine to suggest how good coffee can be evaluated.

Milton Glaser, *Cup of Coffee,* 1973. Courtesy of the artist.

Hyperbole and *transposition* fuel the imagination and visual nonsense of this ceramic artist.

Gifford Myers, *Tasteful Poolside Decor at David's.* Glaze, acrylic on clay, 6" x 6" x 6" (15.2 x 15.2 x 15.2 cm). Gail Severn Gallery, Ketchum, Idaho. Collection of David Hockney.

Hybridization

> With a selected medium, create a hybrid creature or object by "cross-fertilizing" different elements.

Transformation

Change is synonymous with the ongoing characteristics of life, with physiological growth, the intellect, and consciousness. In art, change is the primary motivator of creativity. As a humor-triggering mechanism, transformation is a convivial tool—one that is user-friendly and productive in accordance with the artist's ability to free associate and fantasize.

Thumb-Things

Transform your thumbprints into fanciful creations. Make a series of thumbprints on paper by using a commercial or makeshift ink pad. Add lines, shapes, and designs to transform them into outrageous animals, birds, or alien creatures.

The Transformed Subject

Imagine seeing a subject reflected in a curved mirror that distorts its image. Visualize the image by making a drawing or painting. Other humor-triggering mechanisms to consider: exaggeration or caricature.

Transformed Subject (in 3-D)

Think "What if..." thoughts. What if a chair were constructed of discarded junk or a material never before associated with chair design? Select a commonplace object and imagine it made of unusual materials. Visualize your thought and construct an outrageous three-dimensional object. Other humor triggering-mechanisms to consider: exaggeration, appropriation, or pun.

Glaser: "Surrealism has been an enormous influence on my work as it has been on much of American illustration. This drawing is indebted to Max Ernst and the collages he constructed from old engravings in the thirties."

Milton Glaser, *Flyman,* 1973. Magazine illustration. Courtesy of the artist.

Like Maurits Escher, Farand transforms an ordinary setting into one that is slightly topsy-turvy. The artist makes the cafe's interior "strange" by a calculated distortion of shapes, as if he sees the subject through a glass bottle or reflected in a curved circus mirror.

Mark Farand, *Diner*, 1993. Watercolor. Courtesy of the artist.

I'm trying to be unfamiliar with what I'm doing.
Robert Rauschenberg, b. 1925
American painter

Opposites are used as complementaries rather than contradictions; the result is a formal neutralization that achieves a unique sort of wholeness.

Lucy Lippard, b. 1937
American writer

"Making the familiar strange" is Craig Nutt's motto. "A two-foot-long cayenne pepper makes a remarkable table leg; if you bend a stalk of asparagus just right, it bears an uncanny resemblance to a Queen Anne cabriole leg. The opportunities for historical reference are irresistible as is the impulse to indulge in comic fantasy."

Craig Nutt, *Celery Chair with Peppers, Carrots, and Snow Pea*, 1992. Lacquer on carved wood, leather, 19" x 22" x 37" (48.3 x 55.9 x 94 cm). Photo: Rickey Yanura.

Contradiction

Although at first glance it may seem paradoxical, there is nothing illogical about contradiction, especially as a creative mechanism in art. Great inventions in science and art are brought forth by contradiction and by the momentary chaos that accompanies any search for truly creative ideas or products. As a humor-triggering mechanism, contradiction can powerfully evoke surprise and incongruity—the stuff of wit and humor.

Contradiction Exercise

"What If"

What if the law of gravity were repealed, history were reinvented in a comic mode, or whatever is supposed to be a certain way—isn't? Think up a contradictory situation and visualize it with a material and technique of your choice. Add an exaggeration, reversal, prevarication, or pun to a "what if" situation.

An old nursery rhyme is paraphrased by the artist. Its caption reads "Room for the kids. Older woman retiring. Will trade for condo."

Stan Klyver, *Room for the Kids*, 1986. Pen and ink, 9" x 11" (22.8 x 28 cm). Reprinted with permission of the artist.

Exaggeration

Caricature relies on exaggeration. Jokes, both verbal and visual, rely on exaggeration. Nonsense humor is exaggeration taken to the outer limits and beyond. And because everything new stems from something old, it is safe to say that every creative idea is, in a sense, an exaggeration.

Above:
This pseudohistorical object, reminiscent of Fred Flintstone's appliances, is made of bark sides, a heavy flat gray stone in place of a screen, gut string stretched over the front, and steer antlers for antennae. Zucca: "I like stuff that's not terribly serious—but I'm serious *about* it."

Edward Zucca, *Caveman Television*, 1993. Poplar, hemlock, oak, ash, maple, bark, horn, cowhide, bone, chamois, fieldstone, 74" x 32" x 26" (188 x 81.3 x 66 cm). Peter Joseph Gallery, New York.

Right:
Commercial artist Jose Cruz is particularly noteworthy in his ability to blend design and caricature with a cartoon-style.

Jose Cruz, *Cyndi Lauper*, 1986. Acrylic, airbrush, 13" x 9" (33 x 22.8 cm). Courtesy of the artist.

Exaggeration Exercise 1

Caricature

Try your hand at caricature. Select a family member, a local character or celebrity, or an internationally known personality to depict. Work in pen and ink or a painting medium of your choice, or use clay to make a three-dimensional representation. Exaggerate the features of your subject, but strive to retain the spirit and likeness of the subject.

Exaggeration Exercise 2

Poetic License

Exercise your "poetic license" to reinvent history, create new and irrational specimens of nature, utterly preposterous inventions, chronicles of little-known world records and events, or fanciful pictorializations of curious personalities.

Draw and label your own version of a "little-known botanical specimen." Other mechanisms to bounce your idea against: transposition, transformation, contradiction, parody, pun, narration, or appropriation.

Amiot's ideas for his three-dimensional caricatures emerge from a keen observation of people and social interaction.

Patrick Amiot, *Waitress Scurrying*, 1994. Ceramic, 22" x 8" x 9" (55.9 x 20.3 x 22.8 cm). Courtesy of the artist.

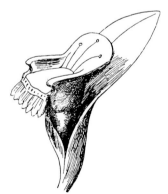

Armchairia Comfortabilis

Crabbia Horrida

Fishia Marina

Cockatooca Superba

Piggiawiggia Pyramidalis

Edward Lear, *Nonsense Botany*, 1871. Left to right: *Armchairia Comfortabilis, Crabbia Horrida, Fishia Marina, Cockatooca Superba, Piggiawiggia Pyramidalis*. Pen and ink. Courtesy of Faber and Faber Limited, London.

With capricious pun-laden humor the artist fashions bizarre wearable costumes for performance art. In the specialized genre of wearable sculpture, Oleszko is a pioneer. Her performances resonate the tradition set by Bauhaus artist Oskar Schlemmer.

Pat Oleszko, *Jazz Mine*, 1994. Mixed media, for clothing design. Courtesy of the artist.

> To exaggerate is to begin
> to invent.
>
> **French proverb**

Exaggeration Exercise 3

Un-doables

Conjure some preposterous, un-doable concepts. Here are two examples from concept artist Don Celender:

- Fill the Grand Canyon with tomato paste.
- Stamp out 100,000 GM cars in the shape of Ralph Nader.

Make a drawing or collage of your ideas.

Parody

Parody pivots on good-natured spoofing. Unlike its venomous cousin, satire, parody seeks only to amuse by the comic interpretation of human nature and its customs, behavior, silly fads, products, icons, and art. Parody is entertainment, pure and simple; its message: "Well, folks, that's life—that's the way it is."

Parody Exercise 1

Archetype

Draw or paint an archetypal personality or character, such as an extrovert, a party animal, politician, recluse, movie star, and so on. Then create a spoof of yourself in a self-portrait. Other mechanisms to consider: caricature, exaggeration, or narration.

Mayer's conception of the pony express is a wacky reconstruction of the American cliché—the horseback postal system that operated across the western United States in the 1860s.

Bill Mayer, *Pony Express*, 1992. Airbrush, gouache, and dyes, 15" x 10" (38.1 x 25.4 cm). Courtesy of the artist.

Parody Exercise 2

Scenario

Draw or paint a parody of a special event or daily activity in the home, school, street, or sports center. Use an exaggerated drawing or cartoon style to make it comic. Create some funny-looking characters and put them in a funny situation. Or select a vegetable, animal, or an object as a subject and anthropomorphize it. Make it parody a human behavior such as reading the morning newspaper, performing in a band, jogging, dancing, romancing, and the like. Model in pottery clay, papier-mâché, or *Sculpey* (a modeling clay that can be baked hard in an ordinary oven). Paint with acrylic colors.

Parody Exercise 3

Single Panel

Parody a human event or situation in a single cartoon panel. Refer to single-panel cartoons in this book or in popular magazines for ideas.

Rodewalt's visual hyperbole implies that the dinosaurs' extinction occurred by careless use of aerosol sprays. Yet, the cartoon tweaks our conscience and reminds us of our collective obligation to guard the world's natural resources.

Vance Rodewalt, *What Ozone Hole?* 1991. Watercolor, brush and ink. *The Calgary Herald.* Reprinted with permission of the artist.

Parody Exercise 4

Shrines, Monuments, and Trophies

Make a funny altar, monument, trophy, or requilary "in honor of" or as a "tribute" to a person, idea, place, or thing. Other humor-triggering mechanisms to think about: caricature, transposition, or appropriation.

Below:
Abrahamson's image paraphrases the animated skeletons *(calavera)* typical of Mexican *Day of the Dead* ceremonial figures.

Kirsten Abrahamson, *Meditatio Mortis*, 1994. Wood, ceramic, mixed media, 3' x 3' x 8" (9.9 x 9.9 x 20.3). Courtesy of the artist.

Left:
The theme paraphrases the old cliché, *One person's junk is another's treasure*. In reconstructing the cliché, the artist has produced a laughable icon that reaffirms the old maxim, "Beauty is in the eye of the beholder."

Richard Newman, *Gorilla Monument: One Man's Kitsch Is Another's Kunst*, 1989. Mixed media, 50" x 32" x 5" (127 x 81.3 x 12.7 cm). Courtesy of the artist.

Pun

Puns can kick-start wonderfully bizarre mental images. From *Acoustic* (what you shoot pool with) to *Zing* (what zider zee zingers do)—the pun is a universally loved form of humor. Granted, it is regarded by some as the lowest form of humor—especially by those who didn't think of it first.

The pun may evolve from topsy-turvy language and word play: homophones (word sound-alikes, such as toe truck instead of tow truck), malapropisms (absurd misuse of words), misspellings, mixed metaphors, and incongruous analogies, spoonerisms (word transpositions, such as "somic trips" for comic strips), and altered phrases (as in artist William Wiley's pun-laden titles, *Nomad Is an Island, Lord Half Mercy, Good Old Daze*).

Pun Exercise 1

Visual Pun

Transform a verbal pun into a visual pun. Start by making a list of words or phrases that have a double meaning, or are malapropisms, altered words, or misspellings. Examples: "car pool," "funny bone," "submarine sandwich," "rule of thumb," "clip joint," "balancing the books," "rung number," "piano tuna," "headquarters," "hindsight," or "flying Dutchman."

Use materials of your choice to make either a drawing, collage, painting, or three-dimensional object.

Pun Exercise 2

Recipe for Making a Riddle

Mike Thaler provided this recipe for making a riddle:

1 Pick a subject, say PIG.
2 Make a list of synonyms and related words: *hog, swine, oink, ham.*

Pat Oleszko's ribald humor and zany puns are part and parcel of her performances. Aside from *Tom Saw-yer*, other themes include: *Udder Delight*, 1990, a multi-teated balloon dress from *Bluebeard's Hassle*; *Pat's Picassos*, 1977, an inflatable costume based on Picasso's *Three Musicians*; *The Clown Jewels*, 1981, a costume that incorporates masks and millinery, a coffee pot, and an Eiffel Tower hat; and *The Coat of Arms*, 1975, a garment sporting twenty-six stuffed arms.

Pat Oleszko, *Tom Saw-yer*, 1985. (Costume for the artist's film, *The Tool Jest*). Photo: Neil Selkirk. Courtesy of the artist.

Puns and word play provide a consistent source of inspiration for Muniz. "Something is funny when perceptions and expectations are short-circuited, when things become opposite to what we imagine them to be, when they free us from conventional wisdom and logic and create spaces in which all learned notions are placed in a suspended state."

Vic Muniz, *Souvenir #60: Flying Dutchman*, 1990. Wooden clogs, roller skate hardware, 4" x 10" x 10" (10.2 x 25.4 x 25.4 cm). Courtesy of the artist.

Never point a pun at a friend—it might be loaded.

John S. Crosbie, b. 1920

Canadian author and pun anthologist

3 Take a word from the list, say HAM. Drop the first letter, H, leaving AM.

4 List words that begin with AM: *ambulance, amnesia, amateur.*

5 Fit the H back on: *hambulance, hamnesia, hamateur.* These are your riddle answers.

6 Now make up your riddle question using the answer's definition:
In what do you take a pig to the hospital? Answer: in a *hambulance.*
What do you call it when a pig loses its memory? Answer: *hamnesia.*
What do you call a pig that's not a professional? Answer: a *hamateur.*

Make up riddles and illustrate them in the form of drawings, cartoons, or sculptures.

Disguise

Disguise is an important mechanism that helps keeps art elusive and free from becoming hackneyed expression. William Wiley made the perceptive remark: "Art is a wonderful concept and one of its main functions is to remain undefined." For many artists, art is like dream work, designed to hide its meaning. René Magritte referred to the vitally important "cloak of obscurity" inherent in his work. The impact of a successful work of art is often achieved by the tension maintained between its mystery and its accessibility to the viewer. This is done by employing both universally understood symbols, to allow viewer access to the work, and personal symbols, which make it ambiguous and maintain its mystery.

High-heeled shoes, flashy guns, pistols as heels, toy poodles on the shoes' insteps, and gaudy color contribute to the comic bizarreness of Buonagurio's work. She gleefully overloads the sculpture with banal forms to raise kitsch to yet greater levels of absurdity.

Toby Buonagurio, *Poodle Puff Gun Shoes, (Guns 'n Poses series)*, 1993. Ceramic, with glazes, lusters, acrylic paint, flocking, glitter, rhinestones, height: 17½" (44.4 cm). Courtesy of the artist. Photo: Edgar Buonagurio.

Disguise Exercise 1

The Disguised Object

Take a derelict, commonplace object such as a telephone, cup, radio, or golf club, and embellish it with ornamentation to the point that it becomes camouflaged. As another possibility, glue colorful beads over its entire surface.

The artist painstakingly covers the entire surface of mundane objects with beads, and in the process, transforms them into fantastic and visually seductive creations. *Beaded Kitchen* is her most ambitious project to date, wherein she has beaded a full-size replica of a household kitchen. Lou: "Maybe I can't change the world, but I can create what I want to look at."

Liza Lou, *Beaded Kitchen*, 1995. Installation. Courtesy of the Natsoulas Gallery, Davis, California.

Disguise Exercise 2

Metaphor

Create a drawing, painting, collage, or assemblage made up of dissimilar elements and images. Use personal symbols, for the most part, which will appeal to a subjective rather than a logical interpretation.

Satire

Like verbal satire, visual satire is biting and acerbic comment. It aims to lay bare the shortcomings, stupidities, and sins of society and to skewer wrongdoers. "The arts, after all," explains critic R. E. Allen, "exist not to explain, but to question; to unearth not the answers, but the possibilities, to remind us of what we can be."

Luzwick's visual satire, like Anne Coe's *Counter Culture*, is couched in humor, though the foreboding message is hard to miss: "Extinction is forever."

Dierdre Luzwick, *Eviction,* 1992. Charcoal on paper. From *Endangered Species*, Harper-Collins, New York, 1992.

> Satire is a sort of [mirror] wherein beholders do generally discover everybody's face but their own.
>
> Jonathan Swift, 1667–1745
> English poet and satirist

Satire Exercise 1

A Seriously Funny View

Locate a news item, or writing in prose or verse, that chronicles an event in which ethical or moral issues are at stake. Topics might include environmental pollution, deforestation, waste disposal, crime, homelessness, unemployment, education, abuse, medicine, disease, and so on. Use the writing to create a satirical drawing, painting, or cartoon that illustrates your point of view on the topic.

Example: "Worldwide, more than one new car is produced every second. Spend the night in bed and when you wake up in the next morning, 30,000 new cars will have been made while you were sleeping."

Satire sans Words

Satirize a particular ethical or moral issue by communicating your idea using only pictures—no words.

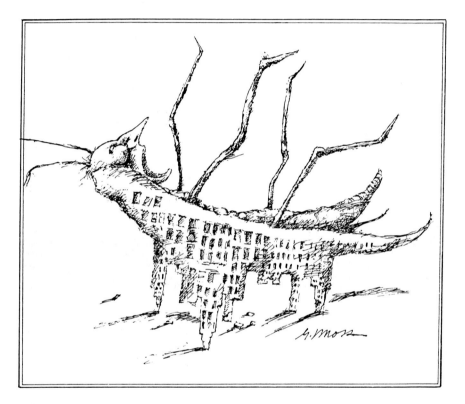

A powerful image that bespeaks urban angst and dysfunction.

Geoffrey Moss, *Untitled (Fallen City)*. Pen and ink. Reprinted with permission of the artist.

Narration

Narrative art—from Egyptian hieroglyphics to Mexican codices and murals, to today's visual arts in all of their forms—is storytelling. Visual narration may be couched in universally understood symbols or in cryptic ones, depending on the artist and circumstance. Narrative art may be whimsical and exist solely for the purpose of entertainment, or it may be didactic, aiming to instruct, guide, or advocate. Picture stories have always figured in world history and are seen in artworks ranging from Bruegel's "visual sermons" to *Peanuts'* comic-strip life parodies.

There are several kinds of stories, but only one difficult one—the humorous.
Mark Twain, 1835–1910
American writer and humorist

143

Stephanie Skalisky, *"R" is for ...Your Relatives* (page taken from her book, *The Alphabet for Extraordinary Children and Eccentric Adults*, 1989). Watercolor, gouache, 11" x 8½" (27.9 x 21.6 cm). Reprinted with permission of the artist and the Michael Himovitz Gallery, Sacramento, California.

Sequenced Imagery

Apply sequenced imagery—images that are arranged in order, so that they communicate an idea, action, or story line. Use the comic strip or book format, or present your narrative in three dimensions by making a tableau or diorama.

Narration Exercise 2

Tribute

Using narration, create a funny award, trophy, or monument as a tribute to a person, idea, object, or place.

Narration Exercise 3

Ilustrated Aphorism

An aphorism is a concise statement of a principle, or a terse formulation of a truth. Select an appropriate aphorism, saying, or adage—or make one up—and illustrate it in a comic style.

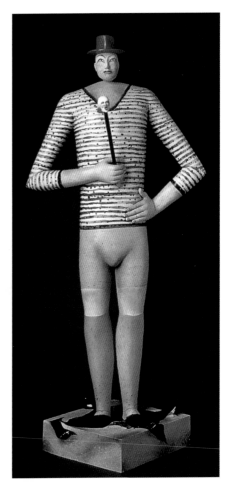

Above:
Warashina's sculpture presents a curious image: a male figure not unlike that of the court jester (or designated fool) holding a curious object—the "talking stick." Aside from punning the word "walking stick," the image recalls the tradition of certain Northwest Indian societies in which the person holding the stick is the designated speaker, a custom put to service in potlatches and ceremonial occasions.

Patti Warashina, *Talking Stick*, 1993. Clay, glaze, 45" x 16½" x 19" (114.3 x 41.9 x 48.3 cm). Bentley Gallery, Scottsdale, Arizona.

Left:
Incorporating numerous clichéd icons, Newman's sculpture echoes a sense of homeyness and patriotism. Veneration or satire?

Richard Newman, *Home Sweet Home*, 1991. Mixed media, 40" x 24" x 24" (101.6 x 61 x 61 cm). Courtesy of the artist.

Appropriation

Sir Joshua Reynolds once remarked, "Nothing comes from nothing." Arguably, nothing can be invented without reference to something else. Scientists build original theories based on previous discoveries, as do artists and inventors. Strictly speaking, progress in art stems in part from the artist's knowledge of art history and world events. It is therefore not an uncommon practice for artists to borrow, paraphrase, quote, or "reinvent" images from past art. The borrowings by contemporary artists are often direct and undisguised, and frequently clothed in impudent humor, satire, and parody.

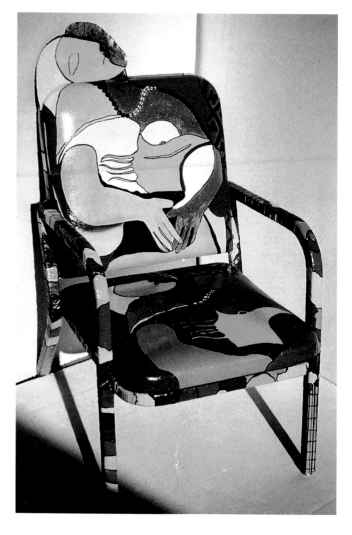

Above:
This work is a whimsical paraphrase of Duchamp's *Nude Descending a Staircase* (1912), and it obliquely berates modern art. It is hilarious in its replacement of the nude figure (the classic symbol of fine art).

David Gilhooly, *Ducks Descending the Staircase (After Duchamp)*, 1991. Ceramic, glaze, 18" x 10" x 22" (45.7 x 25.4 x 55.8 cm). Courtesy of the artist.

Right:
The artist hybridizes two radically different objects, a chair and an image from a painting by Pablo Picasso. The result is an amusing composite of form and function.

Ramona Audley, *Picasso Chair, (Endowed Chairs of the Arts Series)*, 1994. Chair, acrylic color, 36" x 15" x 24" (91.4 x 38.1 x 61 cm). Courtesy of the artist.

Appropriation Exercise 1

Art from Art

Select a reproduction of a well-known work of art to paraphrase. Reinvent it in comic style. Think "what if" thoughts. What if the original image were translated into a cartoon style or changed from its original two-dimensional form into a three-dimensional representation—or into an entirely different frame of reference? For example, a Picasso painting might become a chair, a birdhouse, a mailbox, a design for an automobile or a putting green on a golf course.

Appropriation Exercise 2

Reinventing History and Science

Select a well-known image that celebrates a distinctive moment in history. Change the image (alter history) by introducing a strange presence in the form of a cartoon character or an element from an entirely different domain. Other humor-triggering mechanisms to consider: association, incongruity, absurdity, whimsy, or caricature.

Below:
This narrative relates a pseudohistorical account of a happening in the life of Henri de Toulouse-Lautrec.

Warrington Colescott, *History of Printmaking Series: Lunch with Lautrec*, 1977. Color etching, 22" x 27¾" (55.9 x 70.5 cm). Courtesy of the artist.

Glossary

absurd (n.) That which is irrational, weird, or delightfully nutty, including nonsense imagery, non sequiturs, surrealism.

analogy A comparison between things that are unlike. A means for making humorous relationships between disparate subjects.

anthropomorphism Giving animals or objects human traits.

appropriation Applying aspects—e.g., images, style, overall design—of previously created work to a new creation.

bisociation The incongruous unity of disparate elements; or a frame of mind in which an idea is transferred from one matrix to another, which is governed by a different logic or perspective.

bricoleur One who transforms discarded objects and paraphernalia into a meaningful composition.

burlesque Mockery by ridicule or caricature; imitation in a humorous or derisive manner.

caricature Two- or three-dimensional art in cartoon style that refers to a subject but exaggerates features to a grotesque or ludicrous degree.

cartoon A funny drawing. A term also used to describe animated cartoons or a comic strip.

comics Interconnected pictorial images presented in distinct, sequential frames or panels. Pictorial sequences generally include "speech balloons" or captions to complement the pictorial story line.

double-entendre A figure of speech or an image that possesses a double meaning.

enigmatic The quality of being obscure, mysterious, puzzling, or hard to understand.

equivocal When an image or statement is designed to confuse or mislead, or when it is subject to two or more interpretations.

farcical (from farce) The quality of being ludicrous, laughably inept, or absurd.

figure-ground reversal An optical illusion in which the background and foreground shapes tend to vie for dominance and visually "flip-flop."

free association Connecting thoughts and images from different realms, without restriction; judgment and rationality are held in abeyance.

grotesque Fanciful, bizarre representations in which images or features are distorted to an ugly or absurd result.

humor That quality of expression that appeals to a sense of the ludicrous or absurdly incongruous; the mental facility of discovering, expressing, or appreciating the comical or amusing.

hyperbole An exaggeration, often to a ridiculous degree.

iconography Representation by pictures or images.

idiosyncratic That which is eccentric, off-center, odd, peculiar, strange, erratic, oddball, or weird.

incongruity Something inconsistent with previously known precepts; incompatible ideas, images, objects, situations, or emotions.

irony An incongruity between result and expectation. A depiction opposite to literal meaning; may involve covert sarcasm.

lampoon (v.) To deliver harsh, mocking satire or ridicule, usually directed at an individual or social convention.

metaphor An idea expressed by some form of substitution. A metaphor may contain contradiction but of a logical nature.

narrative A story of an event, real or imaginary, told verbally and/or pictorially. In pictorial narration, such as in the comic strip, various phases of the story are presented in successive panels.

non sequitur A statement or depiction that is not in keeping with what was previously stated. An inference that "does not follow," an absurdity.

oxymoron A self-contradictory figure of speech or image. The term "loud silence" is a literary oxymoron; the image *Self-drawing Hand*, by M. C. Escher, is a visual oxymoron.

paradox That which is self-contradictory, beyond belief, or which seems to hide its meaning.

parody A humorous spoof or "take-off." Mimicry or comic imitation of a selected subject.

prevarication "Telling lies" or untruths for the sake of poetic imagery and comic expression.

pun Humorous word play or image/word play that surprises with sound-alike substitutions to achieve funny and incongruous meaning.

satire Art or literature (or a combination of the two) dedicated to reveal and censure human folly, vice, and stupidity.

slapstick A style of comedy relying on farce, pratfalls, or horseplay.

surreal Beyond reality; a dreamlike depiction. Surrealism as an art movement was founded in 1924 intended to present "the true functioning of thought dictated in the absence of all control exercised by reason."

synaesthesia Sensory crossover. When colors, shapes, forms, and other visual elements are used to represent sound, smell, or taste, or to symbolize mood or emotional states.

synectics A form of creative thinking wherein disparate elements are brought together into unified connection with the notion of producing original and unique structures and/or metaphors.

tomfoolery Nonsense, foolishness.

utopia An imaginary situation or scenario reflecting an impossible, ideal condition.

whimsy A fanciful creation or frame of mind characterized by whims or caprice. An eccentric and funny idea, thought, or image.

wit The ability to relate cleverly seemingly disparate elements so as to illuminate or amuse.

Notes

Chapter One

1 William F. Fry, Jr., address at *The World of Comedy Symposium*, Stanford University, CA, 1978.
2 Murray S. Davis, *What's So Funny?* University of Chicago Press, 1993, p. 7.
3 Ibid.
4 *Handbook of Humor Research*, edited by Paul McGhee and Jeffrey H. Goldstein, Springer-Verlag, NY, 1983, p. 33.
5 Ibid.
6 Arthur Koestler, *The Art of Creation*, Prentice-Hall, 1992.
7 Silvano Arieti, *Creativity—The Magic Synthesis*, Basic Books, NY, 1976, pp. 110–114.
8 William F. Fry, Jr., address at *The World of Comedy Symposium*, Stanford University, CA, 1978.
9 The author's, not necessarily the artist's, interpretation of *Iron Siren*.
10 Mort Gerberg, *Cartooning: The Art and the Business*, William Morrow, NY, 1989, p. 75.
11 Silvano Arieti, *Creativity—The Magic Synthesis*, Basic Books, NY, 1976, pp. 14–15.
12 Ibid, p. 127.
13 Steven Heller, *Graphic Wit: The Art of Humor in Design*, Watson-Guptill, NY, 1991.

Chapter Two

1 Robert M. Polhemus, *Comic Faith*, University of Chicago Press, 1980, p. 7.
2 Humorous visual art has not had a long and cherished kinship with the world of museum curators. However, some major museums have extended their collection policy to include the acquisition of visual humor. These include the Museum of Modern Art and the Whitney Museum, both in New York; the Los Angeles County Museum of Art, the Cleveland Museum of Art; the University of Pennsylvania Museum, Philadelphia; the Stedelijk Museum, Amsterdam; the British Museum and the Tate Gallery, in London; the National Museum of Art, Osaka; the Musée National d'Arte Moderne, and the Centre George Pompidou, in Paris.
3 Donald Kuspit, *Sight Out of Mind*, UMI Research Press, Ann Arbor, MI, 1985, p. xii.
4 Edward-Lucie Smith, *The Art of Caricature*, Cornell University Press, Ithaca, NY, 1981, p. 33.
5 Roger Malbert, *Folly and Vice*, exhibition catalog, Royal Albert Memorial Museum, Exeter, England, 1990.
6 Adam Gopnik, *High and Low: Modern Art, Popular Culture*, Museum of Modern Art, NY, 1990, pp. 179–80. *Marriage a la Mode* is in the National Gallery in London, *A Rake's Progress* is in Sir John Soane's Museum, London, and *Harlot's Progress* was destroyed by fire.
7 Adam Gopnik, *High and Low: Modern Art, Popular Culture*, Museum of Modern Art, NY, 1990, p. 136.

Chapter Three

1 The privilege of uncensored visual speech in the United States should not be taken lightly. Throughout history, artists have been shunned, incarcerated, and even tortured for their outspoken views. It is unfortunate that even today there are still countries in the world that deny freedom of speech to artists. This revealing incident was reported in *Witty World* (Winter/Spring issue, 1994), the international cartoonist magazine. Johnny Hart had no idea that the inno-

cent joke in his "B.C." comic strip (see page 76) would send two Indian editors to a Saudi Arabian prison. Because Saudi officials thought the cartoon questioned the existence of God, the editor for *Arab News*, which allowed the cartoon to be published, was sentenced to two years in prison and 500 lashes. His editor-in-chief received a one-year sentence and 300 lashes. Fortunately, the case received international publicity and the prison sentences were suspended.

2 Arturo Schwarz, *The Complete Works of Marcel Duchamp*, Abrams Publishers, NY, 1970, p. 30.

3 Mort Gerberg, *Cartooning: The Art and the Business*, William Morrow, NY, 1989, p. 43.

4 Charles Baudelaire, *On the Essence of Laughter, and Generally of the Comic in the Plastic Arts*, 1885, in Baudelaire: *Selected Writings on Art and Artists*, trans., P. E. Charvet, Cambridge University Press, 1981.

5 David Featherstone, ed., *Judith Golden: Cycles, A Decade of Photographs*, Friends of Photography, San Francisco, CA, 1988.

6 Susan Sontag, *On Photography*, Farrar, Straus and Giroux, NY, 1978, p. 53.

7 Julia Ballerini, ed., *Sequence (con) Sequence: (Sub)versions of Photography in the 80s*, Edith C. Blum Art Institute, Bard College, 1989.

8 Scott McCloud, *Understanding Comics*, Kitchen Sink Press, Northampton, MA, 1993, p. 74.

9 The Association Internationale du Film d'Animation (ASIFA) was founded in 1960 to organize animation film festivals around the world, such as those that are held at Annecy, Zagreb, and Toronto. A good reference book for further reading is Giannalberto Bendazzi's *Cartoons: One Hundred Years of Cinema Animation*, Indiana University Press, 1994.

Chapter Four

1 Charles Otto Press, *The Political Cartoon*, Fairleigh Dickson University Press, Cranbury, NJ, 1981.

2 Herbert Block, *Herblock: A Cartoonist's Life*, Macmillan, NY, 1993, p. 239.

3 Mary Wortley Montagu, *The Nonsense of Common Sense*, 1737, republished by Northwestern UP, Evanston, IL, 1847.

4 Max Eastman, *Enjoyment of Laughter*, Simon and Schuster, NY, 1936.

5 Paul Conrad in an address to the Association of American Editorial Cartoonists Convention in New Orleans, June 9, 1994.

6 Ralph E. Shikes, *The Indignant Eye*, Beacon Press, Boston, 1969.

Chapter Five

1 Gary Zukav, *The Dancing Wu Li Masters*, William Morrow, NY, 1979.

2 Hendrik van Leeuwen, *Explorations in the Field of Nonsense*, Wim Tiggs, ed., Rodopi, Amsterdam, 1987, p. 83.

3 S. Prickett, *Victorian Fantasy*, Hassocks (Sussex), 1979, pp. 126, 146.

4 Anthony Burgess, Wim Tiggs, ed., *Explorations in the Field of Nonsense*, Rodopi, Amsterdam, 1987, p. 17.

5 Elizabeth Sewell, *The Field of Nonsense*, Norwood Editions, 1977, p. 5.

6 Anthony Burgess, Wim Tiggs, ed., *Explorations in the Field of Nonsense*, Rodopi, Amsterdam, 1987, p. 17.

7 Ibid, introduction.

8 Richard Kostelanetz, *Dictionary of the Avant-gardes*, Chicago Review Press, 1993.

9 *Oxford Companion to Twentieth Century Art*, Oxford UP, 1981, p. 367.

10 Paul Klee, *Pedagogical Sketchbook*, English translation, Faber and Faber, London, 1968.

Chapter Six

1 Send your humorobic exercises, suitable for students or artists of any age, to Nicholas Roukes, c/o Davis Publications, for possible use in future editions of this book.

2 Arieti is a psychologist who wrote *Creativity: The Magic Synthesis*, Basic Books, NY, 1976.

Bibliography

Arieti, Silvano, *Creativity: The Magic Synthesis*. New York: Basic Books, 1976.

Berlyne, D. E., *Laughter, Humor and Play*. Reading, MA: Addison-Wesley, 1969.

Blumenfeld and Alpern, *The Smile Connection*. Englewood Cliffs, NJ: Prentice-Hall, 1936.

Charney, Maurice, *Comedy High and Low: An Introduction to the Experience of Comedy*. New York: Oxford University Press, 1978.

Eastman, Max, *Enjoyment of Laughter*. New York: Simon and Schuster, 1936.

Freud, Sigmund, *The Standard Edition of the Complete Psychological Works of Sigmund Freud. Vol. 8: Jokes and Their Relation to the Unconscious*. London: Hogarth Press, 1986.

Fry, W. F., Jr., *Sweet Madness: A Study of Humor*. Palo Alto: Pacific Books, 1963.

Gerberg, Mort, *Cartooning—The Art and Other Business*. New York: William Morrow, 1989.

Gombrich, Ernst, *Meditations on a Hobby Horse*. New York: Phaidon, 1985.

Goulart, Ron, *The Encyclopedia of American Comics*. New York: Facts on File, 1990.

Gould, Ann, ed., *Masters of Caricature*. New York: Alfred A. Knopf, 1981.

Grotjahn, Martin, *Beyond Laughter*. New York: McGraw-Hill, 1966.

Gruppo Editoriale Fabbri S. A. Milano, *The Arcimboldo Effect*. New York: Abbeville, 1987.

Guilbaut, Serge, *How New York Stole the Idea of Modern Art*. Chicago: University of Chicago Press, 1983.

Haig, Robin Andrew, *The Anatomy of Humor*. Springfield, IL: Charles C. Thomas, 1988.

Heller, Steven, *Graphic Wit: The Art of Humor in Design*. New York: Watson-Guptill, 1991.

—*Man Bites Man*. New York: Watson-Guptill, 1981.

Hess, Stephen and Milton Kaplan, *The Ungentlemanly Art: A History of American Politcal Cartoons*. New York: Macmillan, 1975.

Holland, Norman, N., *Laughing: A Psychology of Humor*. Ithaca, NY, and London: Cornell UP, 1982.

Horn, Maurice, *The World Encyclopedia of Comics*. New York: Chelsea House, 1973.

Hughes, Robert, *Culture of Complaint*. New York: Oxford UP, 1993.

Jacobs, Frank, *The Mad World of William F. Gaines*. Secaucus, NJ: Lylew Stuart, 1972.

Jones, Chuck, *Chuck Amuck: The Life and Times of an Animated Cartoonist*. New York: Farrar, Straus and Giroux, 1989.

Keener, Polly, *Cartooning*. Englewood Cliffs, NJ: Prentice Hall, 1992.

Koestler, Arthur, *The Art of Creation*. London: Hutchinson, 1964.

Kunzle, David, *The Early Comic Strip, Vol., 1*. Berkeley: University of California Press, 1973.

—*The History of the Comic Strip: The Nineteenth Century, Vol. 2*. Berkeley: University of California Press, 1990.

Lear, Edward, *Lear in the Original*. New York: H. P. Kraus, 1975.

Loomans, Diane and Karen Kolberg, *The Laughing Classroom*. Tiburon, CA: H. J. Kramer, 1992.

Lucie-Smith, Edward, *The Art of Caricature*. Ithaca, NY: Cornell UP, 1981.

Marschall, Richard, *America's Great Comic Strip Artists*. New York: Abbeville, 1989.

McCloud, Scott, *Understanding Comics*. Northhampton, MA: Kitchen Sink Press, 1993.

McGhee, Paul E., *Humor: Its Origin and Development*. San Francisco: W. H. Freeman, 1979.

Meglin, Nick, *The Art of Humorous Illustration*. New York: Watson-Guptill, 1973.

Mulkay, Michael, *On Humor: Its Nature and Place in Modern Society*. Cambridge, England: Polity Press, 1988.

Muse, Ken, *The Secrets of Professional Cartooning*. Englewood Cliffs, NJ: Prentice-Hall, 1981.

Nathan, David, *The Laughtermakers: A Quest for Comedy*. London: Peter Owen, 1971.

Perkins, David and Margaret A. Hagen, *Convention, Context, and Caricature*. New York: Academic Press, 1980.

Polhemus, Robert, *Comic Faith*. Chicago: University of Chicago Press, 1980.

Schulze, Franz, *Fantastic Images: Chicago Art Since 1945*. Chicago: Follet Publishing Co., 1972.

Sewell, Elizabeth, *The Field of Nonsense*. Norwood Editions, 1977.

Solomon, Charles, *Enchanted Drawings: The History of Animation*. New York: Alfred A. Knopf, 1989.

Thomas, Bob, *Walt Disney: The Art of Animation*. New York: Simon and Schuster, 1958.

Tiggs, Wim, ed., *Explorations in the Field of Nonsense*. Amsterdam: Rodopi, 1987.

Varnedoe, Kirk and Adam Gopnik, *High and Low: Modern Art and Popular Culture*. New York: Museum of Modern Art, 1991.

Walsh, James, *Laughter and Health*. New York: D. Appelton, 1928.

Zukav, Gary, *The Dancing Wu Li Masters*. New York: William Morrow, 1979.

Raeside is an editorial cartoonist for the *Victoria Times Colonist* in British Columbia. In this cartoon, he satirizes the plight of the farmer.

Adrian Raeside, *Pests,* 1992. Pen and ink. Reprinted with permission of the artist.

Index

About the Author

Prior to becoming a teacher and university art professor, Nicholas Roukes spent several years employed as a commercial artist and cartoonist. During this time he developed a passion for cartooning and a deep curiosity about how comic artists stimulate their imagination for ideas. He also pursued artistic studies including painting, sculpture, architecture, and museum techniques in North America and Europe. He has written extensively about art and served as consulting editor at *SchoolArts Magazine*. Books by Mr. Roukes include: *Kinetic Art, Sculpture in Plastics, Masters of Wood Sculpture, Painting with Acrylics, Acrylics Bold and New, Art Synectics, Design Synectics,* and *Sculpture in Paper*. Presently, he is professor of art emeritus at the University of Calgary, Alberta, Canada.